CONFEDERATE RECORDS

FROM THE

JEFFERSON COUNTY, GEORGIA, COURT OF ORDINARY

By
Michael A. Ports

CLEARFIELD

Printed for Clearfield Company by
Genealogical Publishing Company
Baltimore, Maryland
2015

ISBN 978-0-8063-5763-8

Table of Contents

Introduction

The following transcriptions include both reels of microfilmed Confederate records held by the Jefferson County Court of Ordinary in Louisville and available at the Georgia Department of Archives and History and the Family History Library in Salt Lake City. Some of the original records remain in the offices of the Ordinary, while some have been moved to the state archives in Morrow, Georgia. The first reel is titled *Confederate Soldiers List, Confederate Roster 1861,* and *Miscellaneous Confederate Records,* and contains records from apparently three separate filming efforts. The first filming consists of muster rolls for three volunteer companies of infantry raised in Jefferson County. The second filming is a muster roll of a volunteer company raised in Jefferson County. The third filming consists of muster rolls, rosters, pension rolls, lists of pension applicants, and various letters and other correspondence concerning the veterans and their widows

The second reel, although titled *Pension Roll, 1890*-1952, consists of the county pension rolls from 1890 to 1914. The pension rolls include five distinct and separate lists: disabled or invalid veterans, indigent veterans, indigent veterans in 1910, widows, and indigent widows.

While some of the information also is available in the compiled military service records at the National Archives and Records Administration in Washington, DC and widely available on microfilm and the pension application files held by the Georgia Department of Archives and History, much of the information is available nowhere else. For example, many of the compiled military service records are incomplete, whereas the muster and pension rolls contain detailed information on the soldier's military service, such as date and place of enlistment, promotions, date and place of wounds, date and place of capture, place of confinement, date of exchange, location and service at the close of the war, and date and cause for discharge. One list of invalid pensioners includes detailed a graphic descriptions of the wounds received. The pension rolls sometimes include the date and place of birth and the date of death for veterans and widows who died before 1919, when Georgia began recording death certificates. In addition, the widows pension rolls often include a date and place of marriage.

The original records include both typewritten, printed, and handwritten records. For the most part, the handwriting is legible, making transcription a fairly straightforward process. However, occasional ink blots and smudges, as well as imperfections of the microfilm, individual words could not be deciphered, such occasions noted with brackets, for example [smudge] or [illegible]. The use of _____ indicates a blank space where the clerk never entered the information on the record. The transcriptions of the muster and pension rolls presents dates in a standardized format, spells out all abbreviated place names, corrects incorrectly spelled place names, corrects grammar and punctuation, and abbreviates the ranks of corporal as Corp., sergeant as Sergt., lieutenant as Lt., Junior Second Lieutenant as Jr. 2nd Lt., and lieutenant colonel as Lt. Colonel. No attempt is made to correct the spellings of any names, no matter how obvious the error.

Researchers should consult the microfilm or even the original records to formulate alternative interpretations.

The book is dedicated to the memory of Private Isaac B. Keller, Company H, 63rd Regiment of Georgia Infantry, who served honorably during the entire war, just one of the author's many Confederate ancestors. Many thanks are due the very kind, helpful, and knowledgeable staff at the Georgia Department of Archives and History, who assisted in locating and understanding the context of the records. Thanks also are due Joe Garonzik, of the Genealogical Publishing Company, for his professional advice and counsel. Special thanks are offered to Marcia Tremonti for her encouragement and patience during this challenging endeavor.

List of Confederate Soldiers 1864

The original record volume is typewritten, thus obviously prepared long after the close of the war. The following transcription is from the microfilm made in 1958 by the Genealogical Society of Salt Lake City at the Court of Ordinary in Louisville. The record consists of annotated rosters of three volunteer infantry companies raised in Jefferson County, likely prepared by one or more of the court clerks. The Notes column includes promotions, captures, deaths, wounds, discharges, and other personal information, some of which is not included in the compiled military service records held by the National Archives and Records Administration in Washington, DC. Indicated by italics, the transcription includes the few handwritten notations, apparently later made by a court clerk.

MUSTER ROLL OF COMPANY "C" 20TH REGIMENT, GEORGIA VOLUNTEER INFANTRY, ARMY OF NORTHERN VIRGINIA, C.S.A., JEFFERSON COUNTY.

Name	Rank	Enlisted	Notes
Gamble, Roger L.	Captain	14 Jun 1861	Promoted Major 7 Mar 1862.
Denny, Willis F.	1st Lt.	14 Jun 1861	Promoted Captain 7 Mar 1862
Carswell, Reuben W.	2nd Lt.	14 Jun 1861	Promoted 1st Lt. 7 Mar 1862. Resigned 8 May 1862.
Polhill, Joseph H.	Jr. 2nd Lt.	14 Jun 1861	Resigned 32 Oct 1861.
Jordan, Robert	1st Sergt.	14 Jun 1861	Elected Jr. 2nd Lt. 2 Dec 1861
Peell, William R.	2nd Sergt.	14 Jun 1861	Wounded 20 Sep 1863. Died on account of wound.
Bostick, Patrick N.	3rd Sergt.	14 Jun 1861	Appointed 1st Sergt. Nov 1861.
Carswell, Alexander G.	4th Sergt.	14 Jun 1861	Appointed 3rd Sergt. Dec 1861.
King, James C.	1st Corp.	14 Jun 1861	Appointed 4 Sergt. Dec 1861. Appointed Ordinance Sergt. May 1862.
Jenkins, Jeremiah J.	2nd Corp.	14 Jun 1861	Elected 1 Corp. Dec 1861. Died at Lynchburg, Virginia Hospital 30 Dec 1861.
Poland, Willis C.	3rd Corp.	14 Jun 1861	Elected Lt. 1863.

4

Name	Rank	Enlisted	Notes
Ford, Arthur C.	4th Corp.	14 Jun 1861	Appointed Sergeant-Major of Regiment 1 Sep 1861. Elected Jr. 2nd Lt. 6 Mar 1862.
Adkins, Aaron J.	Private	14 Jun 1861	Transferred 3 Jan 1862 to 28th Ga.
Alexander, David J.	Private	14 Jun 1861	Discharged 16 Nov 1861 by order of Secretary of War.
Amerson, Charles	Private	14 Feb 1863	Died 7 Sept 1864.
Belcher, George W.	Private	14 Jun 1861	Promoted Sergt. Surrendered at Appomattox.
Beal, Christopher C.	Private	14 Jun 1861	
Beall, Samuel S.	Private	14 Jun 1861	Wounded. Surrendered at Appomattox.
Black, Robert E. G.	Private	14 Jun 1861	Elected Lt. 1863. Surrendered at Appomattox.
Brazill, George W. F.	Private	14 Jun 1861	Died at Front Royal, Virginia 6 Feb 1862.
Brown, Patrick M. C.	Private	14 Jun 1861	Wounded.
Brown, Benjamin A.	Private	14 Jun 1861	Promoted to Sergt. Surrendered at Appomattox.
Brown, Edward S.	Private	14 Jun 1861	
Barefield, William	Private	11 Dec 1862	
Barefield, J.	Private		Died in Richmond, Virginia 13 Mar 1863.
Bowen, Zachariah D.	Private	1 Feb 1863	Transferred to 64 Ga Regiment 28 Sep 1864.
Boyle, William	Private	22 Jul 1863	Captured 3 Dec 1863.

Name	Rank	Enlisted	Notes
Brown, Thomas	Private	14 Jun 1861	
Carson, James R.	Private	14 Jun 1861	
Carpenter, David L.	Private	14 Jun 1861	
Clarke, William	Private	14 Jun 1861	Discharged 14 Feb 1863.
Comer, D. M.	Private	1862	Died from wounds.
Coxwell, Washington	Private	14 Jun 1861	
Cheatham, James A.	Private	14 Jun 1861	Died at Manassas, Virginia 15 Aug 1861.
Dixon, Jeremiah T.	Private	14 Jun 1861	Surrendered at Appomattox.
Dunton, H. J.	Private		Lost eye at Hatcher Run, Virginia 1 Oct 1864.
Hasterling, James T.	Private	20 Jun 1861	Discharged 12 Aug 1861, disability.
Edmunds, J. A.	Private		
Edwards, James A.	Private	9 Feb 1863	
Futrel, John A.	Private	14 Jun 1861	
Foster, James R.	Private	13 Feb 1863	Wounded 21 Jul 1864.
Goodwins, William A.	Private	14 Jun 1861	Surrendered at Appomattox.
Green, Wm N.	Private		Furloughed Sick Oct 1864.
Goodwins, Thomas	Private	14 Jun 1861	Died in Jefferson County, Georgia about Dec 1861.
Grubbs, B. A.	Private	14 Jun 1861	Discharged 4 Oct 1861.
Griggs, Thomas H.	Private	9 Feb 1863	
Hannah, William F.	Private	14 Jun 1861	Discharged Apr 1863, furnishing

Name	Rank	Enlisted	Notes
			James Spaulding as substitute.
Hewitt, William C.	Private	14 Jun 1861	Promoted 4th Sergt. 1863. Wounded 19 Sep 1863. Promoted 1st Sergt. Surrendered at Appomattox.
Holt, Thomas	Private	14 Jun 1861	Captured 3 Jul 1863.
Hudson, Alexander M.	Private	14 Jun 1861	
Hudson, Elbert W. W.	Private	14 Jun 1861	
Hazzard, A. B.	Private		Wounded near Richmond, Virginia 1864.
Irwin, Tredwell S.	Private	14 Jun 1861	Discharged 14 Feb 1862, disability.
Isom, William	Private	1862	Served till close of war.
Jordan, Thomas F.	Private	14 Jun 1861	Discharged 2 Dec 1861, disability.
James, J. A.	Private	1861	Served through war.
Jordan, William H.	Private	14 Jun 1861	Died at Manassas, Virginia 3 Aug 1861.
Jones, J. A. F.	Private	1863	Served till close of war.
Jones, Bryant W.	Private	22 Jan 1863	Missing since 3 Nov 1863. Supposed dead.
Key, Joshua F.	Private	14 Jun 1861	Appointed 4th Corp. 2 Dec 1861. Appointed Sergeant-Major of Regiment Mar 1862. Surrendered at Appomattox.
Lefkovich, Leopold	Private	14 Jun 1861	
Lewis, R. R.	Private		
Marshall, Charles	Private	14 Jun 1861	Promoted Corp. Surrendered at

7

Name	Rank	Enlisted	Notes
S.			Appomattox.
McDermott, Andrew	Private	14 Jun 1861	
McWilliams, Robert	Private	1862	Discharged 9 Apr 1865.
McNeely, John P.	Private	14 Jun 1861	
Moxley, Benjamin J.	Private	14 Jun 1861	Detailed as Sergeant of Ambulance Corps Dec 1863. Surrendered at Appomattox.
Murphey, Josiah H.	Private	14 Jun 1861	Surrendered at Appomattox.
Murphey, William T.	Private	14 Jun 1861	
Moxley, William W.	Private	14 Jun 1861	Died 23 Aug 1861 at Manassas, Virginia.
Manson, David H.	Private	22 Jul 1862	Detailed on Division Provost Guard 1863.
McKay, Ephraim D.	Private	22 Jul 1862	Surrendered at Appomattox, Virginia.
McLovin, H. A.	Private		Promoted 1st Lt.
McMulligan, Daniel	Private	22 Jul 1862	
Morris, W. H.	Private		
McWatty, George W.	Private	28 Jul 1864	Wounded 16 Aug 1864. Surrendered at Appomattox.
Outten, George W.	Private	1 Jun 1861	Detailed in Q. M. Dept. 10 Mar 1864
Page, William H.	Private	14 Jun 1861	Discharged at Petersburg, 3 Apr 1865.
Parkes, William R.	Private	14 Jun 1861	Surrendered at Appomattox,

Name	Rank	Enlisted	Notes
			Virginia.
Parker, James R.	Private	14 Jun 1861	
Perdue, Augustus M.	Private	14 Jun 1861	Surrendered at Appomattox, Virginia.
Perdue, Benjamin F.	Private	14 Jun 1861	Died 23 Jan 1862 in camps.
Perkins, Edward W.	Private	14 Jun 1861	
Pilcher, James M.	Private	20 Jul 1861	Wounded 14 May 1864.
Parsons, James H.	Private	14 Jun 1861	Died at Manassas, Virginia 19 Oct 1861.
Raines, William H.	Private	14 Jun 1861	
Roberson, Carlos D.	Private	14 Jun 1861	Discharged 28 Dec 1861.
Rogers, George A.	Private	14 Jun 1861	Discharged Feb 1862, disability.
Rollins, Benjamin F.	Private	14 Jun 1861	Detailed in Laboratory Atlanta, Georgia 5 Oct 1863.
Rooney, Laurence	Private	14 Jun 1861	
Rosier, Stephen W.	Private	14 Jun 1861	
Roberts, John M.	Private	14 Jun 1861	Discharged 7 Jul 1861, disability.
Rollins, Wm A.	Private	14 Jun 1861	Died at Manassas, Virginia 12 Aug 1861.
Scruggs, Joseph L.	Private	14 Jun 1861	Discharged 2 Jan 1862.
Simmons, William J.	Private	14 Jun 1861	Died Sep 1861 at Culpepper, Virginia.
Sinquefield, Perry G.	Private	14 Jun 1861	Died in Richmond, Virginia 29 Apr 1862.
Skinner, W. N.	Private		Died in Richmond, Virginia 17

Name	Rank	Enlisted	Notes
			Mar 1863.
Smith, James R.	Private	14 Jun 1861	Discharged 25 Jan 1862, disability.
Spier, John F.	Private	14 Jun 1861	
Spier, Joseph B.	Private	14 Jun 1861	Appointed 2nd Corp. Dec 1861.
Stephens, Nathan	Private	14 Jun 1861	Discharged 21 Sep 1861.
Scruggs, Richard A.	Private	14 Jun 1861	Died 26 Aug 1861, Manassas, Virginia.
Scruggs, John A.	Private	14 Jun 1861	Died at Manassas, Virginia 4 Aug 1861.
Spaulding, James	Private	30 Apr 1862	Substitute for W. F. Hannah.
Snider, James R.	Private	26 Dec 1862	Captured 3 Jul 1863. Died at Fort Delaware, Delaware 6 Dec 1863.
Tarver, Marcus C.	Private	14 Jun 1861	Died at Lynchburg, Virginia 1 Sep 1861.
Tremble, Joseph L.	Private	14 Jun 1861	Died at Lynchburg, Virginia 1 Sep 1861.
Thaker, D. M.	Private	10 Jun 1861	Supposed died at Manassas, Virginia 1863.
Walden, William G.	Private	14 Jun 1861	Wounded. Surrendered at Appomattox, Virginia.
Walden, George V.	Private	14 Jun 1861	Died at Manassas, Virginia 1861.
Wasden, Alexander	Private	14 Jun 1861	
Walsh, Thomas	Private	14 Jun 1861	
Whitehead, James M.	Private	14 Jun 1861	Died at Culpepper, Virginia 15 Sep 1861.
Wright, James W.	Private	14 Jun 1861	

Name	Rank	Enlisted	Notes
Wright, James F.	Private	14 Jun 1861	Discharged 28 Dec 1861.
Watkins, Rhisa L.	Private	15 Mar 1864	Killed 16 Aug 1864.
Watkins, William W.	Private	25 Sep 1862	Wounded 2 Aug 1864.
Watkins, Littis	Private	18 Feb 1863	

MUSTER ROLL OF COMPANY "H" 63RD REGIMENT.
GEORGIA VOLUNTEER INFANTRY.
ARMY OF TENNESSEE.
C.S.A.
JEFFERSON AND LAURENS COUNTIES, GA.

Name	Rank	Enlisted	Notes
Scranton, H. H.	Captain	20 Dec 1862	Detailed on Court Martial Feb 1864 at Savannah, Georgia.
Polhill, James H.	1st Lt.	20 Dec 1862	Under arrest Feb 1864.
Williams, Thomas F.	2nd Lt.	20 Dec 1862	
Sterling, Edwin M.	Jr. 2nd Lt.	20 Dec 1862	On detached service Feb 1864.
Copps, Chas. J.	1st Sergt.	20 Dec 1862	
Wright, Alexander P.	2nd Sergt.	20 Dec 1862	On detached service Feb 1864.
Campbell, Alexander	3rd Sergt.	20 Dec 1862	Reduced to 4th Corp.14 Mar 1863. Appointed 5th Sergt. June 1863. Died 15 Feb 1864 at Savannah, Georgia.
Pannell, Robert J.	4th Sergt.	20 Dec 1862	Appointed 3rd Sergt. 16 Mar 1863. Reduced to ranks 2 Jun 1863.
Covington, J. W.	5th Segt.	20 Dec 1862	Discharged and furnished substitute Thomas Kearney.
Simon, James	1st Corp.	20 Dec 1862	Appointed 5 Sergt. 5 Jan 1863. Appointed 4th Sergt. Mar 1863, 3rd Sergt. Jun 1863. Transferred to General Hospital, Savannah, Georgia, Oct 1863.
Wilkes, David	2nd Corp.	20 Dec 1862	Appointed 1st Corp. 5 Jan 1863. Reduced to ranks Jun 1863.

Name	Rank	Enlisted	Notes
Henderson, William J.	3rd Corp.	20 Dec 1862	Appointed 2nd Corp. 5 Jan 1863.
Smith, William A.	4th Corp.	20 Dec 1862	Appointed 3rd Corp. 5 Jan 1863. On detached service Jun 1863.
Ambrose, H.	Private	21 Dec 1862	Substitute for James E. Dutton.
Allen, E. C.	Private	Nov 1862	Home of sick furlough close of war.
Amaram, W. D.	Private	21 Dec 1862	Transferred from Company B. On detached service Dec 1862 on Government work Savannah, Georgia.
Brantley, Green J.	Private	2 Dec 1862	Died in Macon, Georgia.
Bush, Chas. G.	Private	2 Dec 1862	Appointed Commissary Jan 1863.
Bush, Frederick	Private	2 Dec 1862	Died in Atlanta, Georgia 29 Jun 1864.
Bush, Henry P.	Private	2 Dec 1862	Transferred to General Hospital Savannah, Georgia Oct 1863. Died Feb 1864 of disease in Laurens County, Georgia.
Bush, William	Private	2 Dec 1862	
Brown, Elijah	Private	2 Dec 1862	Under arrest Feb 1863. Absent without leave Oct 1863.
Bell, James J.	Private	6 Dec 1862	Detailed as cook Jan 1863. Returned to ranks Oct 1863.
Blankenship, H. H.	Private	13 Dec 1862	
Brantley, W. W.	Private	23 Jan 1863	On detached service Jun 1863.
Bass, George W.	Private	3 Feb 1863	
Bracewell, D.	Private	3 Jun 1863	Detailed duty Jul 1863, Whitemarsh Island. Absent

Name	Rank	Enlisted	Notes
			without leave Sep 1863. In arrest Oct 1863.
Burke, H. L.	Private	4 Aug 1863	Detailed duty Jul 1863, Whitemarsh Island.
Beckum, E. D.	Private	4 Aug 1862	Detailed duty Jul 1863, Whitemarsh Island. Died in Augusta Hospital Sep 1864.
Ballard, W. L.	Private	25 Jul 1863	Detailed duty Jul 1863, Whitemarsh Island.
Bones, James W.	Private	18 Sep 1863	On detached service Oct 1863.
Bird, F.	Private	1862	Died at Camp Chase, Ohio 4 Oct 1864.
Bush, T.	Private	29 Sep 1863	Died in Atlanta, Georgia 29 Jun 1864.
Coleman, James L.	Private	29 Dec 1862	Detailed as Musician Jan 1863. Appointed orderly for Colonel Aug 1863.
Cannon, David A.	Private	21 Dec 1862	Absent without leave Feb 1863. Dropped from rolls May 1863. Never reported to Company.
Calhoun, R. M.	Private	21 Dec 1862	Discharged 3 Mar 1863, disability.
Calhoun, J. W.	Private	21 Dec 1862	
Carpenter, J. S.	Private	2 Dec 1862	
Connell, Brazill	Private	1 Dec 1862	Discharged 3 Apr 1863, disability.
Clarke, Henry	Private	2 Dec 1862	Died 22 Mar 1863 at Thunderbolt.
Cooper, P. H.	Private	Oct 1863	In hospital at close of war, sick.
Calhoun, James J.	Private	1 Dec 1862	

Name	Rank	Enlisted	Notes
Calhoun, S. H.	Private	26 Jan 1863	
Calhoun, J. R.	Private	2 Feb 1863	Discharged at Atlanta, Georgia, 1865.
Calhoun, W. J.	Private	10 Feb 1863	
Calhoun, J. J.	Private	1 Dec 1862	
Clements, W. J. S.	Private	21 Dec 1862	Detailed in river picket, Aug 1863.
Clarerty, John	Private	1 Dec 1862	Detailed on Government work in Savannah, Georgia, 1863.
Caughlin, James	Private	10 Jul 1863	Substitute for Andy J. Williams. Deserted 10 Jan 1863.
Curran, John	Private	14 Jun 1863	Appointed Musician Aug 1863.
Chance, M.	Private	14 Aug 1862	
Clarke, F. M.	Private	14 Aug 1862	On detached service Aug 1863. Died in Atlanta, 24 Jun 1864.
Covington, William	Private	10 Aug 1862	On detached service Feb 1864. Detailed in hospital 9 Apr 1865.
Dutton, James R.	Private	13 Dec 1862	Discharged 1 Dec 1862 and furnished substitute, H. Ambrose.
Darby, Jarred	Private	21 Dec 1862	Transferred to General Hospital, Oct 1863, Savannah, Georgia. Served through war.
Douglas, J. A.	Private	30 Dec 1862	
Davis, Thomas	Private	11 Feb 1863	Transferred to Chatham Artillery Mar 1863. Exchanged for J. W. Howard.
Dwyre, M.	Private	31 Dec 1863	Discharged by Commander Post, Savannah, Georgia.

Name	Rank	Enlisted	Notes
Dye, M. G.	Private	20 Aug 1862	Detailed on Whitemarsh Island Aug 1863. Absent without leave Sep 1863. In arrest Oct 1863.
Daniells, S. A.	Private	16 Aug 1863	On detached service Feb 1864.
Daniells, G. W.	Private	16 Aug 1863	
Ellis, N.	Private	21 Dec 1862	
Evans, P.	Private	4 Aug 1863	On detached service Aug 1863.
Furgurson, J. B.	Private	21 Dec 1862	Detailed on Government work in Savannah, Georgia, 1863.
Ford, T.	Private	10 Aug 1863	Transferred to Colonel Wright's Regiment.
Fennell, J.	Private	1862	Discharged at Bentonville, North Carolina Apr 1865.
Graham, A. W.	Private	2 Dec 1862	
Graham, Duncan	Private	13 Jan 1863	Absent without leave Feb 1864. Discharged in South Carolina Apr 1865.
Guann, J. B.	Private	21 Dec 1862	Detailed on Government work in Savannah, Georgia, 1862.
Graham, J. E.	Private	13 May 1863	
Goronto, Jethro	Private	7 Jun 1862	Transferred to Company B, 57 Georgia Regiment, 1 Dec 1863.
Graham, Geo.	Private	14 Sep 1863	Appointed Assistant Cook Oct 1863.
Green, John W.	Private	11 Nov 1863	On detached service Jan 1864.

Name	Rank	Enlisted	Notes
Holmes, William T.	Private	2 Dec 1862	Transferred 30 Sep 1863 to Thompson's Cavalry, in exchange for Hampton Ricks.
Hutchinson, John	Private	Sep 1862	Died Sep 1862.
Hart, Thomas	Private	2 Dec 1862	
Hester, James	Private	2 Dec 1862	
Helton, John	Private	21 Dec 1862	Transferred to General Hospital Oct 1863.
Hutson, James T.	Private	13 Dec 1862	Detailed as picket Aug 1863.
Hobbs, John J.	Private	13 Dec 1862	
Hobbs, Berry	Private	13 Dec 1862	Detailed as Guard Jun 1863, Whitemarsh Island, Georgia.
Hamilton, John	Private	13 Dec 1862	
Hamilton, N. P.	Private	26 Jan 1863	Died 29 Jan 1863, dyptheria.
Hamilton, Irwin	Private	1862	
Hamilton, Thomas	Private	Aug 1862	Discharged Aug 1864.
Howard, William J.	Private	16 Mar 1863	Transferred from Chatham Artillery in exchange for David Thomas. Detailed as clerk in hospital.
Herndon, G. T.	Private	30 Jul 1863	On detached service Aug 1863.
Hall, C. S.	Private	4 Aug 1863	On detached service Aug 1863.
Harrison, Joseph	Private	4 Aug 1863	On detached duty Feb 1864.
Horne, W. W.	Private	2 Jul 1863	
Harrell, Jackson	Private	1862	Surrendered at Greensboro, North

Name	Rank	Enlisted	Notes
			Carolina 26 Apr 1865.
Johnson, James C.	Private	2 Dec 1862	Captured 1863. Detailed as guard at bridge Feb 1864.
Johnson, Thomas	Private	6 Dec 1862	
Jones, J. T.	Private	21 Dec 1862	Detailed on Government work at Savannah, Georgia, 1862.
Jones, L. M.	Private	5 Jun 1863	Detailed river picket, Jun 1863.
Keller, Isaac B.	Private	31 Dec 1862	Detailed wagoner Aug 1863. Furloughed 30 Mar 1865.
Kite, W. W.	Private	26 Jan 1863	Detailed guard Aug 1863, Whitemarsh Island, Georgia. Absent without leave Oct 1863.
Kent, William	Private	26 Jan 1863	Detailed picket Aug 1863.
Kite, R. I.	Private	19 Mar 1863	On detached service Feb 1864.
Kearney, Thomas	Private	27 Dec 1863	Substitute for J. W. Covington. Absent without leave Dec 1862. Deserted 27 Dec 1863.
Lewis, Isaac B.	Private	21 Dec 1862	Detailed as wagoner Jan 1863. Detailed ambulance driver Oct 1863. Discharged 1865 at surrender.
Luckey, William	Private	31 Dec 1862	
Linder, A. T.	Private	7 Jun 1863	Surrendered at Greensboro, North Carolina, 26 Apr 1865.
Livingston, J. O.	Private	4 Aug 1863	
Lampp, W. A., Sr.	Private	22 Dec 1864	Detailed river picket Dec 1864.
Lampp, W. A., Jr.	Private	22 Dec	

Name	Rank	Enlisted	Notes
		1864	
Lane, James W.	Private	22 Dec 1864	
Lafaver, A.	Private	22 Sep 1863	Transferred to Colonel Wright's Regiment.
Murphey, James	Private	21 Dec 1862	
McCry, John	Private	21 Dec 1862	
Molina, R.	Private	22 Dec 1862	Discharged 1 Mar 1863, disability.
Mimms, John	Private	3 Jul 1863	Absent without leave Sep 1863. Killed at Kennesaw, 1864.
Musland, W. H.	Private	2 Sep 1863	Detailed in Ordinance Department Sep 1863.
McNeil, John M.	Private	30 Sep 1863	Detailed as Orderly's clerk Oct 1863.
Oliver, T. A.	Private	13 Dec 1862	
Oliphant, T. A.	Private	13 Dec 1862	Appointed 4th Corp. Jun 1863. Appointed Color Corp. Jan 1864.
Olmstead, E. H.	Private	3 May 1863	
Perry, Eason	Private	13 Dec 1862	
Pope, Jackson	Private	2 Dec 1862	Detailed as cook Jan 1863.
Parker, F. L.	Private	3 Feb 1863	Detailed as cook Jan 1863. Transferred to McAlpin's Company 17 Sep 1863.
Pannell, R. J.	Private	15 Nov 1863	

19

Name	Rank	Enlisted	Notes
Register, Jeff.	Private	6 Dec 1862	Discharged from hospital close of war.
Register, J. P.	Private	13 Dec 1862	Died at Savannah, Georgia hospital 16 Sep 1863.
Rowland, James	Private	13 Dec 1862	
Ricks, Hampton	Private	6 Aug 1863	Transferred from Thompson's Cavalry in exchange for W. T. Holmes.
Rowland, Joseph	Private	Dec 1862	Died in Savannah, Georgia hospital Aug 1863.
Rickeson, M.	Private	5 Aug 1863	
Smith, S. K.	Private	29 Jul 1863	Transferred to Genral Hospital at Savannah, Georgia Oct 1863. Died Nov 1863.
Smith, E. A.	Private	1 Aug 1863	Died of measles Sep 1864.
Samples, Wm D.	Private	21 Dec 1862	Absent without leave Jan 1863. In arrest Oct 1863
Samples, Robert M.	Private	21 Dec 1862	Discharged 10 Apr 1863, disability.
Stevens, D.	Private	30 Jan 1863	
Sheppard, J. R.	Private	16 Feb 1863	
Spivey, William	Private	22 Dec 1862	
Scott, John	Private	28 Feb 1863	Appointed Musician Jan 1864.
Smith, W. T.	Private	21 Dec 1862	Detailed on Government Works in Savannah, Georgia 1862.
Sullivan, J.	Private	19 Dec 1862	Substitute for J. B. Dutton. Transferred to Company B.

Name	Rank	Enlisted	Notes
Sumner, J. M.	Private	7 Jun 1863	
Stewart, J. D.	Private	7 Jun 1863	Transferred to General Hospital, Savannah, Georgia Oct 1863.
Stevens, Berry	Private	1 Jun 1863	Transferred to General Hospital, Savannah, Georgia Oct 1863.
Stevens, Nathan	Private	25 Feb 1863	Detailed on Whitemarsh Island Aug 1863.
Turner, George B. H.	Private	6 Dec 1862	Died in Louisville, Kentucky 28 Jun 1864.
Thompson, J. P.	Private	21 Dec 1862	Detailed as cook Jan 1863.
Taylor, Henry	Private	9 May 1863	
Williams, Andy J.	Private	6 Dec 1862	Discharged 10 Jan 1863 and furnished a substitute Jas. Caughlin.
Williams, William	Private	21 Dec 1862	
Williams, Dennis B.	Private	21 Dec 1862	
Wright, W. E.	Private	21 Dec 1861	Died 13 Jun 1863.
Wambles, J. W.	Private	15 Dec 1862	Appointed river picket Jan 1863.
Wingood, J. B.	Private		Died at Camp Chase, Ohio 20 sep 1864.
Wilkes, Alexander	Private	13 Dec 1862	
Willis, Joseph B.	Private	8 Dec 1862	Appointed 1st Corp. 5 Jan 1863. On detached service Feb 1864.
Watson, James	Private	6 Dec 1862	Detailed in hospital Oct 1863.

Name	Rank	Enlisted	Notes
Warnick, D.	Private	2 Dec 1862	
Wilkes, David	Private	18 Dec 1862	
Wilkins, W. A.	Private	22 Jan 1863	Appointed guar Aug 1863. Died in Lagrange, Georgia Jun 1864.
Wright, M.	Private	16 Feb 1863	
Williams, J. P.	Private	30 Jan 1863	Died 26 Feb 1863 at Thunderbolt Hospital.
Wilkes, A. P.	Private		Wounded.
Wright, M. C.	Private	1862	Home on sick furlough close of war.
Wilkins, J. C.	Private	3 Feb 1863	Appointed 5th Sergt. Mar 1863. Appointed 4th Sergt. Jun 1863.
White, J.	Private	19 Aug 1863	Detailed on Whitemarsh Island Aug 1863. In arrest Oct 1863.
Wilkes, Elijah	Private	7 Nov 1863	
Young, C. W.	Private	31 Dec 1862	Absent without leave Feb 1863. Detailed to picket Aug 1863. Wounded.
Youngblood, J.	Private	10 Aug 1863	

MUSTER ROLL OF COMPANY I, 28TH REGIMENT.
GEORGIA VOLUNTEER INFANTRY.
ARMY OF TENNESSEE.
C.S.A.
JEFFERSON COUNTY, GA.

Name	Rank	Enlisted	Notes
Cain, James G.	Captain	10 Sep 1861	Promoted Major 13 Nov 1861, Lt. Colonel 3 May 1862. Wounded at Malvern Hill, Virginia 1 Jul 1862. Dropped from prolonged absence without leave. Restored 28 Mar 1863. Resigned account of wound.
Adkins, Isaac F.	1st Lt.	10 Sep 1861	Promoted Captain 13 Nov 1861. Resigned account of ill health 15 Apr 1862.
Stapleton, James	2nd Lt.	10 Sep 1861	Promoted 1st Lt. 13 Nov 1861, Captain 19 Apr 1862. Resigned account of ill health 28 Jan 1863.
Pugesley, A. J.	Jr. 2nd Lt.	10 Sep 1861	Promoted 2nd Lt. 13 Nov 1861. Resigned account of ill health 5 Jul 1862.
Douglas, William H.	1st Sergt.	10 Sep 1861	Promoted J. 2nd Lt. 13 Nov 1861, 1st Lt. 19 Apr 1862. Wounded at Malvern Hill, Virginia 1 Jul 1862. Promoted Captain 28 Jan 1863. Resigned account of ill health and wound.
Cain, George L.	2nd Sergt.	10 Sep 1861	Promoted 1st Sergt. 13 Nov 1861, Jr. 2nd Lt. 12 Jul 1862, 1st Lt. Jan 1863.
Lockhart, A. J.	3rd Sergt.	10 Sep 1861	~~Died in service in 1862~~. *Residing in Florida.*
Wren, J. J.	4th Sergt.	10 Sep 1861	Died in service 17 Apr 1862 at Yorktown.

Name	Rank	Enlisted	Notes
Stephens, M. B.	5th Sergt.	10 Sep 1861	Died in service at Richmond, Virginia Dec 1862.
McKigney, J. F.	1st Corp.	10 Sep 1861	Died in service in at Richmond, Virginia 1861.
Harvey, W. R.	2nd Corp.	10 Sep 1861	Promoted 2nd Sergt.
Walden, E. M.	3rd Corp.	10 Sep 1861	Promoted 2nd Lt.
Williams, J. L.	4th Corp.	10 Sep 1861	Promoted 1st Sergt. Jan 1863. Served till close of war.
Adkins, A. J.	Private	10 Sep 1861	Promoted Corp. Jan 1863. Served till close of war.
Adkins, Aaron J.	Private	15 Aug 1862	
Aldred, A. R.	Private	10 Sep 1861	
Aldred, David	Private	10 Sep 1861	Discharged 1861. Furnished E. Eubanks as substitute.
Aldred, J. M.	Private	10 Sep 1861	Died of disease at Manassas, Virginia 1861.
Aldred, William N.	Private	10 Sep 1861	
Anderson, Daniel	Private	1 Oct 1864	Exchanged for W. G. Williams. Discharged at Greensboro, North Carolina 26 Apr 1865.
Beall, W. H.	Private	Feb 1864	In hospital at Greensboro, North Carolina, close of war.
Blankenship, W. K.	Private	10 Sep 1861	Died of disease 22 July 1862.
Brassell, J. H.	Private	10 Sep 1861	Died in service 22 Jul 1862.
Brickle, D. H.	Private	10 Sep 1861	Died in service 28 Jul 1862 at Richmond, Virginia.
Clarke, James	Private	10 Sep 1861	

Name	Rank	Enlisted	Notes
Coleman, R. H.	Private	10 Sep 1861	*Died in Alabama since the war.*
Coleman, W. N.	Private	10 Sep 1861	Died of disease at Manassas Junction, Virginia, 1861.
Copelan, J. M.	Private	4 Aug 1863	
Covington, Francis	Private	10 Sep 1861	Died at Richmond, Virginia, 1861.
Covington, V. E.	Private	10 Sep 1861	Detailed in Pioneer Corps, 1863. Discharged Apr 1865 at Bushill, North Carolina.
Denton, David	Private	10 Sep 1861	Wounded at Mechanicsville, Virginia26 Jun 1862. 2nd Lt. Jan 1863. Resigned account of wound, 1863.
Dixon, Nehemiah	Private	27 May 1864	Surrendered 1865.
Dye, R. S.	Private	10 Sep 1861	Died of disease in Richmond, Virginia 1862.
Eubanks, E.	Private	1861	Substitute for David Aldred.
Fountain, Allen	Private	10 Sep 1861	Wounded at South Mountain, Maryland14 Sep 1862, Wounded at Ocean Pond, Florida 20 Feb 1864. Died of wound.
Gorman, Mark	Private	10 Sep 1861	Substitute for J. R. Lyon.
Guy, J. A.	Private	10 Sep 1861	Discharged account of disease 1862.
Haddon, Edmond	Private	10 Sep 1861	Died of disease 1862.
Haddon, G. W.	Private	10 Sep 1861	Wounded at South Mountain, Maryland 14 Sep 1862. Killed at Chancellorsville, Virginia 3 may 1863.
Haddon, Jasper	Private	10 Sep 1861	Killed at Fort Sumter, South Carolina 1863.

Name	Rank	Enlisted	Notes
Haddon, John W.	Private	3 Mar 1862	Died of disease in Richmond, Virginia 1862.
Haddon, N. J.	Private	3 Mar 1862	Killed at Cold Harbor, Virginia 3 Jun 1864.
Haddon, Samuel	Private	10 Sep 1861	Wounded at Sharpsburg. Maryland 17 Sep 1862. Killed at Ocean Pond, Florida 20 Feb 1864.
Haddon, Wm Jasper	Private	3 Mar 1862	Killed at Fort Sumter, South Carolina Nov 1863.
Haddon, W. P.	Private	3 Mar 1862	Died at Richmond, Virginia hospital Aug 1862.
Hall, B.	Private	1861	Substitute for J. O. Spann.
Hannah, William	Private	10 Sep 1861	Discharged account of disease. *J. L. Hannah.*
Harvey, H. *J.*	Private	10 Sep 1861	*Still living 1906. 1936.*
Headen, James C.	Private	10 Sep 1861	
Henderson, *L.*	Private	10 Sep 1861	*Still living 1906. Died Washington County, Georgia.*
Hobbs, W. D.	Private	3 Mar 1862	Surrendered at Greensboro, North Carolina.
Holmes, H. H.	Private	10 Sep 1861	*Still living 1906.*
Holmes, W. H.	Private	10 Sep 1861	Wounded at Chancellorsville, Virginia 3 May 1863.
Irby, J. A.	Private	10 Sep 1861	Captured at Sharpsburg, Maryland 17 Sep 1862. Exchanged Oct 1862.
Irby, W. R.	Private	10 Sep 1861	Promoted Corp. Jan 1863. Discharged at Greensboro, North Carolina 1865.
Kinnebrew, C. J.	Private	10 Sep 1861	Died of disease at Manassas

Name	Rank	Enlisted	Notes
			Junction, Virginia 1861.
Lafavor, James W.	Private	10 Sep 1861	Captured at South Mountain, Maryland 14 Sep 1862.
Lafavor, J. T.	Private	10 Sep 1861	Wounded and captured at South Mountain, Maryland 14 Sep 1862.
Lazenby, Frank	Private	May 1864	Killed at Cold Harbor, Virginia 3 Jun 1864.
Tiffany, A. J.	Private	10 Sep 1861	Wounded at Bentonville, North Carolina 19 Mar 1865 and died of wound.
Tiffany, A. S.	Private	10 Sep 1861	Appointed Regimental Color Bearer. Killed at Ocean Pond, Florida 20 Feb 1864.
Loyd, H. J.	Private	28 Sep 1863	
Lyon, J. R.	Private	10 Sep 1861	Discharged Aug 1862. Furnished Mark Gorman as substitute.
Lyon, J. W.	Private	10 Sep 1861	Transferred to 27th Georgia Regiment 1861.
McCrackin, J. R.	Private	10 Sep 1861	Killed at Fort Harrison, Virginia Oct 1864.
McKingney, J. W.	Private	10 Sep 1861	Died of disease in Richmond, Virginia 1861.
Martin, Allen	Private	28 Sep 1863	
Mathis, Ennis	Private	10 Sep 1861	
Minton, Joshua	Private	28 Aug 1862	
Mulling, Thomas E.	Private	10 Sep 1861	Died of disease at Manassas Junction, Virginia 1861.
Mathews, M. F.	Private	May 1864	Discharged at Augusta, Georgia Apr 1865.

Name	Rank	Enlisted	Notes
Peebles, Ebin	Private	10 Sep 1861	Killed at Fort Harrison, Virginia Oct 1864.
Peebles, James M.	Private	10 Sep 1861	
Peebles, J. M.	Private	10 Sep 1861	Wounded at Petersburg, Virginia May 1864. At home close of war.
Peeler, James	Private	10 Sep 1861	Died of disease at Richmond, Virginia 1861.
Perdue, R. N.	Private	10 Sep 1861	Promoted Corp. Jan 1863. Killed at Fort Harrison, Virginia Oct 1864.
Perdue, William	Private	10 Sep 1861	Killed at Petersburg, Virginia May 1864.
Perkins, Richard	Private	10 Sep 1861	Promoted Sergt. of Litter Corps
Pope, B. B.	Private		Lost one finger.
Pervis, G. M.	Private	10 Sep 1861	
Pophand, G.	Private	10 Sep 1861	Died in Richmond, Virginia 24 May 1864.
Pugesley, W. H.	Private	10 Sep 1861	Appointed Assistant Surgeon.
Roberson, D. D.	Private	10 Sep 1861	Died of disease in Richmond, Virginia 1861.
Roberson, William	Private	3 Mar 1862	Sick in 1863.
Ragsdale, W. A.	Private		Wounded 9 Jul 1864.
Roberson, W. F.	Private	10 Sep 1861	Detailed as ambulance driver, 1862.
Robinson, Dempsey	Private	Aug 1861	Died of disease 22 Feb 1862.
Shepherd, Elijah	Private	10 Sep 1861	Wounded at Mechanicsville, Virginia 26 Jun 1862. Died of wound in Richmond, Virginia31

Name	Rank	Enlisted	Notes
			July 1862.
Shepherd, Green	Private	10 Sep 1861	Wounded at Petersburg, Virginia Jul 1864. Died of wound Aug 1864.
Shepherd, J. *Frank*	Private	10 Sep 1861	Died of disease at Manassas Junction, Virginia 1861. *Married Becky Hadden. Parents of Mrs. Joe F. Sheppard, Stapleton, Georgia. Mrs. Lizzie Padgett born in 1859.*
Smith, A. F.	Private	26 Apr 1862	Promoted Jr. 2nd Lt. Jan 1863.
Span, J. O.	Private	10 Sep 1861	Discharged 1861. Furnished B. Hall as substitute.
Stapleton, G. L.	Private	25 Aug 1862	
Stapleton, Thomas A.	Private	25 Aug 1862	Killed at Fort Harrison, Virginia Oct 1864.
Stapleton, William	Private	10 Sep 1861	
Sturnes, M. B.	Private	10 Sep 1861	Died in Richmond, Virginia 1 Oct 1862.
Taff, G. F.	Private	10 Sep 1861	Died in Richmond, Virginia Mar 1863.
Thigpen, H. J.	Private	3 Mar 1862	
Thompson, J. G.	Private	10 Sep 1861	
Thompson, S. A. H.	Private	10 Sep 1861	Wounded at Sharpsburg, Maryland 17 Sep 1862.
Thompson, W. R.	Private	10 Sep 1861	Discharged. Furnished substitute.
Thompson, Geo. W.	Private		Served through war.
Thompkins, S. A.	Private	27 Mar	Substitute for J. K. N. Walden.

Name	Rank	Enlisted	Notes
R.		1862	
Vause, J. M.	Private	10 Sep 1861	Wounded at Fredericksburg, Maryland 13 Dec 1862.
Vause, W. A.	Private	10 Sep 1861	Wounded at Petersburg, Virginia 30 Aug 1864, and lost leg. Discharged.
Vause, W. D.	Private	3 Mar 1862	Missing at Sharpsburg, Maryland 17 Sep 1862.
Walsh, R. J. N.	Private	10 Sep 1861	Captured at South Mountain, Maryland 14 Sep 1862.
Walden, K. J. N.	Private	10 Sep 1861	Discharged 1861. Furnished S. A. R. Thompkins as substitute.
Whiteley, J. N. P.	Private	10 Sep 1861	
Wilkinson, Jesse	Private	10 Sep 1861	
Williams, James L.	Private	3 Mar 1862	Promoted Corp. Jan 1863. Wounded at Bentonville, North Carolina 19 Mar 1865. Discharged at Augusta, Georgia.
Williams, J. F.	Private	3 Mar 1862	In prison Mar 1865.
Williams, R. A.	Private	10 Sep 1861	
Williams, R. W.	Private	10 Sep 1861	Detailed in Pioneer Corps. Served to close of war.
Williams, S. A.	Private	3 Mar 1862	Wounded at Sharpsburg, Maryland 17 Sep 1862. Discharged at Greensboro, North Carolina Apr 1865.
Williams, T. J.	Private	10 Sep 1861	Died of disease at Manassas Junction, Virginia 1861.
Williams, W. O.	Private	10 Sep 1861	Transferred to Cavalry 1864 in exchange for D. Anderson.

Name	Rank	Enlisted	Notes
Willoughby, John	Private	10 Sep 1861	Missing at Sharpsburg, Maryland 17 Sep 1862. Killed at Cold Harbor, Virginia 3 Jun 1864.
Willoughby, N. A. J.	Private	10 Sep 1861	Killed at South Mountain, Maryland 14 Sep 1862.
Wood, R. A.	Private	3 Mar 1862	Wounded at Kingston, North Carolina 1863.
Wilkinson, R. N.	Private	Aug 1861	Discharged at Bush Hill, North Carolina 1865.

Confederate Roster 1861

The original volume consists of a roster of a local volunteer militia company known as the Jefferson Grays, later incorporated into the 28th Georgia Infantry Regiment as Company I. The transcription is from the microfilm made in 1958 by the Genealogical Society of Salt Lake City in the offices of the Court of Ordinary in Louisville. While the roster clearly is labeled with the year 1861, there is no indication that the roster was made or even begun in 1861, although the latter is the more likely case.

The roster, a pre-printed ledger, apparently to document the recruitment of local militia companies, consists of a table with ten columns titled Name, Time of Enlistment, Rank, Promoted To, When and to What Command Transferred, Discharge Caused of, Died When and How, Captured When and Where, Exchanged When, and Name of Battles in which Engaged During Service. The roster, while substantially incomplete, contains information not included in the compiled military service records held by the National Archives and Records Administration in Washington, DC.

The transcription consists of a table with four columns, Name, Rank, Promoted To, and Notes, combining the remaining information in the last column. The first 77 names on the roster all enlisted in August 1861, no enlistment date entered for the remaining names. Starting with R. A. Williams, the last twenty names have the word Recruit in the column headed Time of Enlistment, implying that those men were not original members of the militia company, but recruited later. The 28th Georgia Volunteer Infantry Regiment was organized at Big Shanty, Georgia, during July and August, 1861, recruiting its members from Irwin, Sumter, Washington, Crawford, Cherokee, Stewart, Toombs, Jefferson, and Emanuel Counties. In June 1862, the Confederate Army assigned the regiment to Colquitt's Brigade.

A clerk, possibly an original member of the company, handwrote the underlined information at the head of the roster. The first thirteen names on the roster include both the original commissioned and noncommissioned officers, in order of rank, followed by the 84 privates in nearly alphabetical order by surname.

Roster of <u>Jefferson Greys</u>, a Company Organized or Recruited from <u>Jefferson County</u>, Georgia, <u>Walden's Church, July 1861</u>, Which Company was known as <u>I</u>, No. of Regiment of Georgia <u>28th</u>, Brigade <u>Colquit's</u>, <u>Army of Northern Virginia</u>.

Name	Rank	Promoted to	Notes
James G. Cain	Captain	Lt. Colonel	Wounded 1 Jul 1862 Malvern Hill. Resigned Wound. Seven Pines, Cold Harbor, Mechanicsville, Malvern Hill.
Isaac F. Atkins	1st Lt.	Captain	Resigned Ill Health
James Stapleton	2nd Lt.	Captain	Resigned Ill Health
A. J. Pugesly	3rd Lt.		Resigned Ill Health
Wm Douglass	1st Sergt.	Captain	Wounded 1 Jul 1862 Malvern Hill. Discharged from wound. Ill Health. Died Disease. Petersburg, Fort Harrison, Fisher, Kingston, Bentonville, Mechanicsville, Cold Harbor, Malvern Hill, Wagner, Ocean Pond.
George L. Cain	2nd Sergt.	1st Lt.	Fort Fisher, Kingston, Bentonville, Sharpsburg, Chancellorsville, Wagner, Ocean Pond, Petersburg, Fort Harrison, Mechanicsville, Cold Harbor, Malvern Hill, South Mountain.
A. J. Lockhart	3rd Sergt.		
J. J. Wren	4th Sergt.		
M. B. Stephens	5th Sergt.		Died 1861 Richmond, Virginia.
J. F. McKigney	1st Corp.		Died 1861 Richmond, Virginia.
W. R. Harvey	2nd Corp.	Sergt.	In all the above named battles with Douglas & G. L. Cain.
E. M. Walden	3rd Corp.	2nd Lt.	In all the above named battles with Douglas & G. L. Cain.
J. L. Williams	4th Corp.	1st Sergt.	In all the above named battles with Douglas & G. L. Cain.

33

Name	Rank	Promoted to	Notes
Aldred, J. M.	Private		
Aldred, A. R.	Private		
Aldred, D. W.	Private		
Boswell, J. H.	Private		
Brassell, Jas.	Private		Died 1861 Richmond, Virginia.
Brockle, D. H.	Private		
Coleman, W. M.	Private		
Coleman, R. H.	Private		
Covington, Francis	Private		
Covington, V. E.	Private		
Dye, R. S.	Private		
Denton, David	Private		
Holmes, H. H.	Private		
Harvey, H. J.	Private		Fort Harrison, Fort Fisher, Kingston, Sharpsburg, Chancellorsville, Wagner, Ocean Pond, Petersburg, Mechanicsville, Cold Harbor, Malvern Hill, South Mountain.
Irby, W. R.	Private		Fort Harrison, Fort Fisher, Kingston, Sharpsburg, Chancellorsville, Wagner, Ocean Pond, Petersburg, Mechanicsville, Cold Harbor, Malvern Hill, South Mountain.
Irby, J. A.	Private		
McCrackin, J. R.	Private		
Perdue, W^m	Private		Fort Harrison, Fort Fisher, Kingston, Sharpsburg, Chancellorsville, Wagner, Ocean Pond, Petersburg, Mechanicsville,

Name	Rank	Promoted to	Notes
			Cold Harbor, Malvern Hill, South Mountain.
Perdue, R. M.	Private		
Pervis, L. M.	Private		
McKinna, Jas.	Private		
Kinnabrue, C. G.	Private		
Henderson, L.	Private		
Halden, Edmond	Private		
Hadden, W. P.	Private		
Lafaver, J. W.	Private		
Lafaver, J. T.	Private		
Robinson, D. D.	Private		Died 1861 in Richmond, Virginia Disease.
Robinson, Frank	Private		
Robinson, W. F.	Private		Ambulance Driver.
Perkins, Richard	Private		
Thompson, J. G.	Private		
Thompson, W. R.	Private		
Vause, W. A.	Private		Wounded 30 Aug 1864 Petersburg, Virginia. Discharged Wound. Sharpsburg, Chancellorsville, Wagner, Ocean Pond, Petersburg, Mechanicsville, Cold Harbor, Malvern Hill, South Mountain.
Vause, J. M.	Private		Sharpsburg, Chancellorsville, Wagner, Ocean Pond, Petersburg, Mechanicsville, Cold Harbor, Malvern Hill, South Mountain.

Name	Rank	Promoted to	Notes
Wilkerson, Jesse	Private		
Willerby, M. A. J.	Private		
Williams, T. J.	Private		
Williams, R. W.	Private		
Williams, W. G.	Private		Exchanged for D. Anderson. Transferred to the Cavalry 1864.
Willerby, John	Private		
Matthews, Ennis	Private		
Span, J. O.	Private		
Hannah, W^m	Private		
Lyon, J. R.	Private		
Lyon, J. W.	Private		
Walden, K. J. N.	Private		
Blankinship, W. K.	Private		
Whitely, J. W. P.	Private		
Fountain, Allen	Private		
Tifney, A. S.	Private		
Tifney, A. J.	Private		
Groman, Mark	Private		
Sheppard, Elijah	Private		
Sheppard, J. T.	Private		
Thompson, S. A. H.	Private		
Adkins, A. J.	Private		

Name	Rank	Promoted to	Notes
Peebles, J. M.	Private		Wounded May 1864 Petersburg, Virginia. Sharpsburg, Chancellorsville, Petersburg, Mechanicsville, Cold Harbor, Malvern Hill, South Mountain.
Peebles, Ervin	Private		
Clark, Jas.	Private		
Guy, J. A.	Private		
Mullin, T. E.	Private		Discharged 1861 Disease.
Puler, J. M.	Private		
Roberson, W^m	Private		
Williams, R. A.	Private		
Williams, S. A.	Private		
Williams, J. F.	Private		
Williams, Jas. L.	Private		
Wood, R. A.	Private		
Hadden, N. J.	Private		
Hadden, G. W.	Private		
Hadden, Samuel	Private		
Hadden, John	Private		
Hadden, Jasper	Private		
Loyd, H. J.	Private		
Martin, V. A.	Private		
Stapleton, Thos.	Private		
Stapleton, W	Private		

Name	Rank	Promoted to	Notes
Hobbs, W. D.	Private		
Smith, A. F.	Private		
Thigpen, A. J.	Private		
Vauce, J. Daniel	Private		
Lazenby, A. J.	Private		
Beall, W. H.	Private		

Miscellaneous Confederate Records

In 1958, the Genealogical Society of Salt Lake City microfilmed a variety of bound and loose Confederate records held by the Jefferson County Ordinary. The records primarily consist of company rosters, ledgers, lists of veterans and pensioners, pension rolls, correspondence, and other loose papers.

Confederate Veterans List 1893

The original record consists of a handwritten ledger, containing two lists of Confederate veterans, the first apparently made of veterans residing in Jefferson County in 1893, and the second of denied pension applications dated 1910. In the upper right margin of the first page, the clerk entered the notation, *"Too Much Property Mostly,"* apparently indicating the reason for denial of most of the applications. Following the two lists, court clerks recorded the winners of various agricultural prizes, probably at a succession of county fairs, but those records are not transcribed here.

1. E. A. Blackwell, 2nd South Carolina Cavalry Regiment, Captain Chestnut

2. Chas. Allen, 62nd Georgia Regiment Cavalry, J. B. Jones Captain

3. M. H. Hopkins, 1st Volunteer Regiment of Georgia, Colonel C. H. Olmstead

4. A. L. Patterson, Grov. Scout, 1836

5. J. H. Beckworth, 48th Georgia, Captain Kelly

6. S. J. McNair, 48th Georgia, Co. E., Captain Cheatham

7. H. J. Hudson, 38th Georgia, Co. G., Captain W. H. Batty

8. Daniel Anderson, 28th Georgia, Co. I, Captain W. H. Douglass

9. J. W. Lafeaver, 28th Georgia, Co. I, Captain W. H. Douglass

10. W. E. Penrow, Cobb's Legion, Co. F, Captain M. D. Jones

11. James Atwell, Smith Division

12. G. H. Harrell, 29th Georgia, Co. A, B. M. M.

13. F. A. Sinquefield, Co. F, Cobb's Legion, Cavalry

14. S. R. Raburn, Co. A, 48th Georgia, Captain Kella

15. W. A. Willie, 1st Regiment Florida

16. W. A. Vause, Co. I, 1st Georgia Regiment

17. D. B. McGinnis, Co. C, 45 Regiment Alabama Volunteers

18. J. J. Walsh, Co. B, 59th Georgia

19. T. H. Smith, Co. G, 58th Georgia

20. L. H. Cook, Co. H, 14th Georgia

21. N. W. Bedingfield, Co. E, 48th Georgia

22. R. J. Greenway, Co. G, 57th Georgia

23. J. J. Whigham, Co. B, 27th Georgia, Batt.

24. George Miller, 8th Georgia Cavalry

25. Amos Walden, Co. C, 54th Georgia

26. M. P. Lake, Co. F, Jeff Davis Legion

27. W. A. Brown, Co. G, 38th Georgia

28. J. W. Jones, Co. E, 48th Georgia

29. W. Screws, Co. E. 48th Georgia

30. A. G. Carswell, Co. C, 20th Georgia

31. Ellis Johnson, Co. B, 59th Georgia

32. J. H. Upton, Co. I, 11th Georgia

33. G. M. Bedingfield, Co. I, 2nd Georgia Batt.

34. W. H. Page, Co. C, 20th Georgia

35. V. A. Powell, Co. E, 48th Georgia

36. J. T. Wilson, Co. B, 28th Georgia

37. R. A. J. Kitchens, Co. B, 28th Georgia

38. J. M. Cherry, Co. E, 5th Georgia Reserves

39. A. R. Rountree, Co. E, 15th Alabama

40. J. W. Cheatham, Co. E, 48th Georgia

41. A. H. Warlten, Co. D., 5th Georgia

42. W. H. Douglass, Co. G, 28th Georgia

43. James Gordon, Co. F, Cobb's Legion, Cavalry.

44. R. H. Chaplier, Co. B, 1st Georgia

45. G. W. Kindrick, Co. E, 48th Georgia

46. P. W. Raiford, Co. H, 2nd Georgia

47. J. W. Black, Co. E, 48th Georgia

48. H. J. Bedingfield, Co. E, 48th Georgia

49. W. D. Moxley, Co. E, 48th Georgia

50. J. H. Cotter, Co. E, 48th Georgia

51. B. Fennel, Co. E, 48th Georgia

52. L. F. Berry, Co. C, 49th Georgia

53. Z. D. Bowen, Co. C, 20th Georgia

54. M. H. Beull, Co. I, 28th Georgia

55. J. H. Culpepper, Co. D, 5th Georgia

56. W. R. Thompson, Co. I, 28th Georgia

57. J. M. McGahee, Co. E., 8th Georgia Cavalry

58. A. A. Murphy, Co. G, 38th Georgia

59. W. W. Fleming, Co. L, Cobb's Legion

60. J. W. Tucker, Co. A., 63rd Georgia

61. Elijah Gordon, Co. F, Cobb's Legion

62. T. G. Beasley, Co. E, 27th Georgia, Batt.

63. W. J. Rogers, Co. E, 27th Georgia, Batt.

64. W. G. Walden, Co. C, 20th Georgia

65. A. S. Moxley, Co. B, 22nd Georgia Battl.

66. J. L. Scruggs, Co. L, Cobb's Legion, Cavalry

67. W. M. Woods, Co. A,

68. W. B. Adams, Co. E, 48th Georgia

69. J. R. Rollins, Co. D

70. W. G. Sammons, Co. A, 48th Georgia

71. W. J. Quincy, Co. K, 20th Georgia

72. Lenny McNeely, Co. A, 20th Georgia

73. J. T. Glover, Sr., Co. B, 22nd Georgia

74. T. E. Walden, Co. B, 60th Georgia

75. E. Palmer, Co. E, Cobb's Legion

76. Joel Guy, Co. H, 12th Georgia Ball.

77. E. M. Averet, Co. B, 2nd Georgia Militia

78. I. B. Kelley, Co. H, 63rd Georgia

79. H. W. Hall, Co. E, 48th Georgia

80. A. G. Powell, Co. E, 48th Georgia

81. Z. J. Clackton, Co. E, 48th Georgia

82. T. E. Swan, Co. G, 38th Georgia

83. C. S. Wise, Co. G, 38th Georgia

84. S. L. Cowart, Co. L, Cobb's Legion

85. J. A. Fleming, Co. L, Cobb's Legion

86. D. J. Grubbs, Co. C, 54th Georgia

87. J. E. Futral, Co. E, 48th Georgia

88. U. Anderson, Jackson Artillery

89. G. R. Allen, Co. G, 57th Georgia

90. A. B. Oats, Co. F, Cobb's Legion

91. R. A. Deihl, Co. D, 1st Georgia

92. T. M. McNeely, Co. E, 48th Georgia

93. L. B. McDaniel, Co. E, 48th Georgia

94. W. F. Atkinson, Co. G, Battery Guiard, 38th

95. Curran Becton, Co. B, 1st Bttn. Georgia Sharpshooters

96. M. A. Carswell, Co. B, 2nd Georgia Reserves

97. R. W. Stephens, Co. B, Smith's Battalion

98. B. J. Brown, Co. B, 27th Georgia

99. J. B. Dawson, Co. F, Cobb's Legion

100. Berry Hall, Co. F, Cobb's Legion

101. J. H. Coleman, Howell's Battery

102. R. J. Jones, Co. E, 38th Georgia

103. J. S. Rogers, Co. G, Battery Guiard

104. W. J. Henderson, Co. H, 63rd Georgia

105. J. A. Smith, Co. B, 27th Georgia Battalion

106. W. E. Meade, Howell's Battery

107. Geo. T. Verderey, Co. B., 21st Georgia

108. Thos F. Jordan, Co. C, 20th Georgia

109. W. R. Harvey, Co. I, 28th Georgia

110. J. J. Thompson, Co. G, 38th Georgia

111. S. H. Scarborroh, Co. K, 28th Georgia

112. A. H. Sammins, Co. B, 22nd Georgia

113. S. A. H. Thompson, Co. I, 28th Georgia

114. J. H. Brantly, Co. F, 62nd Georgia

115. W. F. Way, Co. G, 38th Georgia

116. J. J. Reynolds, Co. F, Cobb's Legion

117. G. A. Lambert, Co. F, Cobb's Legion

118. G. G. Johnson, Co. F, Cobb's Legion

119. N. J. Moxley, Co. F, Cobb's Legion

120. W. H. Johnson, Co. F, Cobb's Legion

121. T. J. Tant, Milledge Artillery

122. E. M. Drake, Co. E, 38th Georgia

123. C. J. Fields, Co. F, 8th Georgia Cavalry

124. G. F. Underwood, Co. F, 8th Georgia Cavalry

125. J. P. Thompson, Co. H, 63rd Georgia

126. B. B. Pope, Co. I, 28th Georgia

127. G. W. McWatty, Co. C, 20th Georgia

128. J. J. Polhill, Co. B, 27th Battalion

129. F. A. Pendy, Co. F, 8th Georgia Cavalry

130. J. B. Stewart, Co. G, 38th Georgia

131. A. S. Smith, Co. G, 38th Georgia

132. Dr. J. M. Johnson, Co. T, Cobb's Legion

133. J. R. Smith, Co. E, 48th Georgia

134. A. W. Aldred, Co. E. 48th Georgia

136. J. W. Weeks, Co. G, 38th Georgia

138. W. D. Hunter, Co. B, 10th Georgia

139. W. S. Thompson, Co. F, 8th Georgia Cavalry

140. J. F. Postin, Co. F, 8th Georgia Cavalry

141. J. M. Kennedy, Co. F, Cobb's Legion

142. Willis Hall, Simm's Brigade

143. J. W. Brinsin, Co. G, 38th Georgia

144. J. W. Reynolds, Co. D, 2nd Georgia

145. P. M. Brown, Co. C, 20th Georgia

146. J. B. Watkins, Stapleton's Company

147. S. J. Gordon, Co. F, Cobb's Legion

148. J. S. Oury, Co. F, 3rd Georgia

149. J. M. Jones, Co. D, 1st Georgia

150. L. D. Johnson, Co. F, Cobb's Legion

150. Ben Beasley, Co. G, 38th Georgia

151. L. B. Clay, Co. G, 13th Tennessee

152. B. A. Grubbs, Co. C, 1st Georgia

153. D. W. Aldred, Co. I, 28th Georgia

154. H. L. Burke, Scranton's Company

155. W. C. Matthews, Co. G, 38th Georgia

156. S. E. McNeely, Co. D, 27th battalion

157. M. H. Paradise, Co. G, 57th Georgia

158. G. W. Quinsey, Co. B, 27th Battalion

159. A. R. Aldred, Co. I, 28th Georgia

160. A. J. Hall, Co. D, 2nd Georgia Battalion

161. J. J. Keith, Latimore's Battery

162. S. J. Bowen, Co. H, 2nd Georgia

163. R. A. Stone, Wright's Brigade

164. W. J. Clements, Co. H, 63rd Georgia

165. J. L. Lafalie, Co. A, 48th Georgia

166. D. J. Thompson, Co. B, 27th Georgia Battalion

167. J. H. Rhodes, Co. D, 12th Georgia Battalion

168. J. K. Kinman, Co. D, 12th Georgia Battalion

169. J. P. Fleming, Co. F, Cobb's Legion

170. J. S. Walea, Co. K, 28th Georgia

171. E. D. Alman, Co. F, 62 Georgia Cavalry

172. E. Alman, Co. D, 54th Georgia

173. Lewis Brown, Cobb's Legion

174. Jarvey Hall, Co. C, 20th Georgia

175. T. J. James, Co. B, 12th Georgia

176. W. B. Johnson, Co. F, Cobb's Legion

177. G. L. Cain, Co. I, 28th Georgia

178. J. C. Little, Co. F, 8th Georgia Cavalry

179. T. A. Jones, Co. H, 14th Georgia

180. W. J. Blackstone, Joe Brown

181. B. J. Moxley, Co. C, 20th Georgia

182. J. M. Jordan, Co. F, 8th Georgia Cavalry

183. R. W. Williams, Co. D, 28th Georgia

184. W. S. Danforth, Batt. Artillery

185. T. J. Aldred, Co. H, 22nd Georgia

186. Hardy Hall, Militia

187. Jacob Jones, Co. D, 1st Georgia

188. S. M. Clark, Co. B, 27th Georgia Battalion

189. A. P. Horn, Co. E, Marine Corps

190. Jas. Rountree, Co. F, Cobb's Legion

190. G. J. Barrwick, Co. l, Cobb's Legion

191. M. L. Brown, Co. L, Cobb's Legion

192. B. W. Durden, Co. L, Cobb's Legion

193. Rufus Cross, Co. L, Cobb's Legion

194. T. J. Sharp, Co. B, 14th Georgia

195. J. W. Whigham, Co. H, 2nd Georgia

196. W. R. Peel, Co. C, 20th Georgia

197. C. W. Young, Co. H, 63rd Georgia

198. J. R. Perry, Co. I, 2nd Florida

199. G. W. McKenzie, Co. H, Bowen's Brigade

200. M. Newman, Adjt., 49th Georgia

201. Sid A. Pughesly

202. W. Y. Brown, Co. E, 48th Georgia

203. R. B. Crawford, Co. K, 48th Georgia

204. J. B. Smith, Co. E, 27th Georgia Battalion

205. W. H. Bowen, Co. A, 3rd Georgia

206. W. J. Stevens, Co. F, 14th Georgia

207. Angus Boyd, Co. G, 2nd South Carolina

208. Asa Brown, Co. E, 48th Georgia

209. Demis Robbins, Co. D, 47th Georgia

210. J. L. Rains, Co. D, 27th Georgia Battalion

211. J. S. Mills, Co. A, 3rd South Carolina

212. J. G. Cain, Lieutenant Colonel, 28th Georgia

213. J. M. Johnson, Co. F, Cobb's Legion

214. W. H. Johnson, Co. F. Cobb's Legion

215. E. M. Dike, Co. G, 38th Georgia

Applications Turned Down 1910

Willis Arrington, Co. G, 12th Georgia Infantry

W. G. Brown

D. A. Cannon, 1st Georgia Regulars, Co. C

G. M. Dabbs, Co. B, 1st Battalion Tennessee Volunteers

Jas. E. Daniel, Co. H, 12th Georgia Regiment Cavalry

S. S. Galphin, Co. C, 1st South Carolina Cavalry

R. C. Gay, Co. I, 48th Georgia

D. R. Green, Co. K, 28th Georgia Volunteers, Colquitt's Brigade

Robert Hatcher, Co. B, 19th South Carolina

A. P. Jones, 2nd South Carolina Regiment Light Artillery

R. J. Jones

Thos. F. Jordan, Co. C, 20th Georgia Regiment & Co. O, 48th Georgia, Wright's Brigade & Co. C, 38th Georgia, Gordon's Brigade

J. P. Kendrick, Co. G

A. D. La Favor, Co. H, 63rd Regiment Infantry, 12th Georgia Cavalry, not six months service straight

Lawson B. McDaniel, Co. E, 48th Georgia Volunteers, Wright's Brigade

Denny McNeely, Co. A, [faint] Carpenters

Thos. H. McNeely, Co. E, 48th Regiment Georgia Volunteers

John D. Ponder, Co. C, 1st Georgia Regulars, wife Elizabeth

S. C. Purvis, Co. B, 48th Regiment Georgia Volunteers

J. T. Reid, 38th Regiment, Joe Thompson Artillery

Jesse Reese, Co. A, 22nd Georgia, Warren County Militia

49

J. W. Roberts, Co. B, 27th Georgia Battalion

James A. Screws,

Amanda J. Smith,

John E. Steedy, Co. G, 1st Regiment South Carolina Volunteers

W[m] R. Thompson, Co. F, 2nd Georgia Cavalry

Jesse Young, Co. G, 38th Georgia Infantry, S

1. James S. Atwell

2. Amos Walden

3. J. H. Coburn

4. Ba. J. Sailthens

5. W. A. Stevens

6. C. Perkins

7. W. Farehand

8. P. Perkins

9. W. G. Scruggs

10. Jesse Lockhert

11. B. G. Moxley

12. G. W. Quinney

13. J. W. Jones

14. S. R. Tarver

15. L. F. Berry

16. W. Q. Arrington

17. J. J. Sewel

18. A. J. McNeely

19. E. J. Attaway, MD

20. Y. K. Hobbs

21. J. L. Scruggs

22. J. T. Cross

23. S. H. Culpepper

24. T. [ink blot]

25. G. H. Harrell

26. L. B. McDaniel

27. W. E. Clark

28. A. R. Aldred

29. Ellis Johnson

30. C. A. Matthews

31. R. L. Bargainise

32. W. S. Danforth

33. R. W. Underwood

34. Angos Boyd

35. V. A. Powell

36. B. Fennel

37. W. A. Tarver

38. B. S. Carswell

39. W. E. Purvis

40. A. J. M. Jordan

41. T. M. McNeely

42. R. G. Swift

43. G. W. Clark

44. Jas. J. Clark

45. A. G. Carswell

46. J. M. Underwood

47. J. R. Ross

48. W. J. Blackston

49. [ink blot] W. Harden

50. F. Hannah

51. M. Rereirister

52. L. H. Cook

53. J. E. Futral

54. J. F. Upton

55. S. J. Hall

56. C. L. Reese

57. B. J. Brown

58. W. B. Beasley

59. L. J. Futral

60. J. L. Rains

61. R. M. Holmes

62. E. H. Fields

63. W. A. Barton

64. E. Tahirgn

65. B. B. Belcher

66. G. M. Bedingfield

67. S. M. Aldridge

68. B. A. Grubbs

69. A. E. Oglesby

70. C. J. Sheppherd

71. G. R. Allen

72. J. H. Beckworth

73. J. W. Brassell

74. H. B. Clemens

75. M. G. Scruggs

76. D. H. Swan

77. E. W. Way

78. T. A. McBride

79. F. A. Martin

80. W. J. Douglass

81. J. W. Brinson

82. Jno. D. H. Alexander

83. W. A. Johnson

84. E. M. Drake

85. W. B. Francis

86. A. C. McKay

87. W. E. Means

Roster Company I, 28th Georgia Infantry Regiment

The original handwritten roster consists of a printed ledger having eleven columns titled Name, Time of Enlistment, Rank, Promoted to, When and to What Command Transferred, When and Where Wounded, Discharged Cause of, Died When and How, Captured When and Where, Exchanged When, and Name of Battles in which Engaged During the War. The following transcription includes all of the listed information in five columns, combing much of the listed information in the Notes column.

Roster of Jefferson Greys, a Company Organized or Recruited from Jefferson County, Georgia, Walden's Church, July 1861, Which Company was known as I, No. of Regiment of Georgia 28th, Brigade Colquitt's, Army of Northern Virginia.

Name	Enl.	Rank	Promoted to	Notes
E. Eubanks	1862	Private		Substitute
H. J. Lloyd	1863	Private		
V. A. Martin	1863	Private		
B. B. Pope	1863	Private		
Daniel Vause	1862	Private		
Jefferson Copling	1863	Private		
A. F. Smith	1863	Private	3rd Lt.	
Thompkin	1862	Private		Substitute
Joshua Minton	1862	Private		
Thos. Gay	1864	Private		
Goun Phillips	1864	Private		
Moses Russell	1864	Private		
Walter Stapleton	1864	Private		
Berry Hall		Private		Substitute
W. D. Hobbs	1862	Private		
James G. Cain	Aug	Captain	Lt. Colonel	Wounded 1 Jul 1862 Malvern Hill.

Name	Enl.	Rank	Promoted to	Notes
	1861			Resigned Wound.
Isaac F. Atkins	Aug 1861	1st Lt.	Captain	Resigned disease.
James Stapleton	Aug 1861	2nd Lt.	Captain	Resigned disease
A. J. Pugesly	Aug 1861	3rd Lt.		Resigned Ill Health
Wm Douglass	Aug 1861	1st Sergt.	Captain	Wounded 1 Jul 1862 Malvern Hill.
George L. Cain	Aug 1861	2nd Sergt.	1st Lt.	
A. J. Lockhart	Aug 1861	3rd Sergt.		Discharged due to disease.
J. J. Wren	Aug 1861	4th Sergt.		Died from disease Manassas 1861.
M. B. Stephens	Aug 1861	5th Sergt.		Died from disease Manassas 1861.
J. F. McKigney	Aug 1861	1st Corp.		Died from disease Manassas 1861.
W. R. Harvey	Aug 1861	2nd Corp.	Sergt.	
E. M. Walden	Aug 1861	3 Corp.	2nd Lt.	
J. L. Williams	Aug 1861	4th Corp.	1st Sergt.	
Aldred, I. M.	Aug 1861	Private		Died from disease Manassas 1861.
Aldred, W. W.	Aug 1861	Private		
Aldred, A. R.	Aug	Private		

Name	Enl.	Rank	Promoted to	Notes
	1861			
Aldred, D. W.	Aug 1861	Private		
Boswell, J. H.	Aug 1861	Private		Died from disease Manassas 1861.
Brickle, D. H.	Aug 1861	Private		Died from disease Richmond, Virginia1862.
Coleman, W. M.	Aug 1861	Private		Died from disease Manassas 1861.
Coleman, R. H.	Aug 1861	Private		
Covington, Francis	Aug 1861	Private		Died from disease Manassas 1861.
Covington, V. E.	Aug 1861	Private		
Dye, R. S.	Aug 1861	Private		Died from disease Richmond, Virginia1862.
Denton, David	Aug 1861	Private		Wounded Mechanicsville Jun 1862. Resigned due to wound.
Holmes, H. H.	Aug 1861	Private		
Harvey, H. J.	Aug 1861	Private		
Irby, W. R.	Aug 1861	Private		
Irby, J. A.	Aug 1861	Private		

Name	Enl.	Rank	Promoted to	Notes
McCrackin, J. R.	Aug 1861	Private		Killed Fort Harrison 1864.
Perdue, William	Aug 1861	Private		Killed Petersburg 1864.
Fountain, Allen	Aug 1861	Private		Killed Ocean Pond 1864
Tiffany, A. S.	Aug 1861	Private	Color bearer of the regiment.	Killed Ocean Pond 1864.
Tiffany, A. J.	Aug 1861	Private		Killed Bentonville 1865.
Shepperd, Grun	Aug 1861	Private		Wounded Petersburg 1864. Died from wound 1864.
Shepperd, Elijah	Aug 1861	Private		Wounded Mechanicsville 1862. Died from wound 1862.
Shepperd, J. T.	Aug 1861	Private		Died from disease Manassas 1861.
Adkins, A. J.	Aug 1861	Private	Corporal	Wounded Petersburg 1864.
Peebles, J. M.	Aug 1861	Private		Wounded Petersburg 1864. Discharged for wound 1864.
Clark, James	Aug 1861	Private		
S. A. H. Thompson	Aug 1861	Private		
J. A. Guy	Aug 1861	Private		Discharged for disease 1861.
Mullins, Thomas E.	Aug 1861	Private		Died of disease Manassas 1861.

Name	Enl.	Rank	Promoted to	Notes
Williams, R. A.	Aug 1861	Private		
Peeler, J. M.	Aug 1861	Private		Died of disease Manassas 1861.
Williams, S. A.	Mar 1862	Private		
Williams, Jas. L.	Mar 1862	Private		
Williams, J. F.	Mar 1862	Private		
Wood, R. A.	Mar 1862	Private		Wounded Ocean Pond 1864.
Thigpen, A. J.	Mar 1862	Private		
Hadden, Samuel	Mar 1862	Private		Killed Ocean Pond 1864.
Hadden, Gurn	Mar 1862	Private		Killed Chancellorsville 1863.
Hadden, Jasper	Mar 1862	Private		Killed Fort Sumter 1863.
Hadden, N. J.	Mar 1862	Private		Killed Cold Harbor 1864.
Hadden, John	Mar 1862	Private		Died from disease Richmond 1862.
Peebles, Ebin	Mar 1862	Private		Killed Fort Harrison 1864.
Stapleton, Thomas	Nov 1862	Private		Killed Fort Harrison 1864.
Stapleton, William	Nov 1862	Private		

58

Name	Enl.	Rank	Promoted to	Notes
Lazenby, Frank	1864	Private		Killed Cold Harbor 1864.
W¹ H. H. Beall	1864	Private		Captured Kinston, 1864.
Anderson, Daniel	1864	Private		Transferred from cavalry for W. G. Williams.
Gorman, Mark	1862	Private		Substitute for J. R. Lyon
Perdue, R. N.	Aug 1861	Private		Killed Fort Harrison 1864.
Pervis, L. M.	Aug 1861	Private		
McKigney, James	Aug 1861	Private		
Kinabrew, C. J.	Aug 1861	Private		
Henderson, L.	Aug 1861	Private		
Haddon, Edmond	Aug 1861	Private		
Haddon, W. R.	Aug 1861	Private		
Lafaver, J. W.	Aug 1861	Private		
Lafaver, J. T.	Aug 1861	Private		Wounded South Mountain 1862.
Pugesley, W. H.	Aug 1861	Private	Assistant Surgeon	
Robinson, D. D.	Aug 1861	Private		

Name	Enl.	Rank	Promoted to	Notes
Robinson, Frank	Aug 1861	Private	Ambulance Driver	
Perkins, Richard	Aug 1861	Private	Litter Carrier	
Thompson, J. G.	Aug 1861	Private		
Thompson, W. R.	Aug 1861	Private		
Vause, W. A.	Aug 1861	Private		Wounded Petersburg 1864.
Vause, J. M.	Aug 1861	Private		
Wilkerson, Jesse	Aug 1861	Private		
Willoughby, John	Aug 1861	Private		Killed Cold Harbor 1864.
Willoughby, M. A. J.	Aug 1861	Private		Killed South Mountain 1862.
Williams, T. J.	Aug 1861	Private		
Williams, R. W.	Aug 1861	Private		
Williams, W. G.	Aug 1861	Private		Exchanged for D. Anderson. Transferred to the Cavalry 1864.
Mathis, Ennis	Aug 1861	Private		
Span, J. O.	Aug 1861	Private		
Hannah, William	Aug	Private		

Name	Enl.	Rank	Promoted to	Notes
	1861			
Lyon, J. R.	Aug 1861	Private		
Walden, K. J. N.	Aug 1861	Private		
Blankenship, W. K.	Aug 1861	Private		
Whitely, John W.	Aug 1861	Private		

Pensions Under Act of General Assembly Passed December 19th 1900

The original handwritten list appears to be on one out-sized sheet of paper, ruled into twelve untitled columns, presented here in a table of eight columns. In spite of being untitled, the contents of all of the original columns appear straightforward. The first column is the name of the pensioner. The second column probably indicates how long the pensioner had lived in Georgia. Every entry in the third column is Ga., so it is not repeated here. Because every entry in the fourth column is Private, the rank column also is not repeated here. The fifth column is the company designation. The transcription combines the sixth and seventh columns into one indicating the regiment. The eighth column is the brigade. The ninth and tenth columns are combined into one indicating the place and state where the veteran was wounded. The eleventh column is the date the veteran received the wound. The final twelfth column is a description of the wound. Unlike all of the other records on the microfilm roll, the quality of the image for this document is very poor and difficult to read.

P. M. Brown	Life	C	20 Ga	Benning	Gettysburg, Pennsylvania	3 Jul 63	Was shot in the left arm at the wrist & running upward. Remains a ruin & sore to this day
S. R. Raburn	Life	A	48 Ga	Wright	Malvern Hill, Virginia	6 Jul 62	Minie ball passing through left hand and trimming all the fingers away
H. J. Hudson	Life	G	38 Ga	Gordon	Spotsylvania Court House, Virginia	12 May 64	Shot in the left groin with minie ball which produced lameness and has affected him for
E. Palmer	Life	E	Cobb's Legion				Was wounded at ___ River, North Carolina by being
Green J. Bell	Life	G	57 Ga		Jackson, Mississippi	16 May 63	By a piece of shell on the right leg near the ankle which produced a running sore which has disabled me for years

	Life	I	1st Ga	Garnett			In the right side of the right lung, ball entered through 3rd rib & ranged down near the spine
E. J. Gaines	Life	F	8 Ga Cav	Daniell		23 Jun 64	Was shot under the right nipple with a minie ball & coming out under the shoulder blade, causing constant hiccoughing
Jerry Howard	1840 Life	G	38 Ga	Gordon	On picket duty, Atlanta	18 May 62	When guarding Government stores, was shot in left hand & arm, bursting hand & arm half way to elbow
W. A. Vause	Life	I	28 Ga	Colquitt	Petersburg, Virginia	30 Jul 64	Was wounded in the left leg, which was afterward amputated just below the knee
W. A. Brown	Life	G	38 Ga	Gordon	Winchester, Virginia	10 Sep 64	Ball entered left wrist and ____ which still remains in that condition
J. M. Thomas	Life	L	Cobb's Legion		Hagerstown, Maryland	12 Jul 63	Wounded in right arm at elbow & part of bone taken out, which leaves arm stiff & unfit for use
E. M. Higgins	1837	B	59 Ga		Sharp shooter at Petersburg, Virginia	15 Jun 64	Was shot in the right shoulder, cap of shoulder shot off
C. W. James, Jr.	1828	H	63 Ga	Mercer	Kennesaw Mountain	2 Jul	Minie ball passed through left foot just below the

63

						64	ankle, which bursted the foot all to pieces
Adaline Rowland	Life	H	14 Ga				My husband took sick with the measles and died when in the service at Hurtsville, Virginia. Witnesses: T. D. Smith, Ben Adkinson, & Harvey Smith
J. G. Lively	Life	H	48 Ga	Wright	Second Manassas, Virginia		Was wounded in left hand & had three fingers amputated.
Curran Becton	Life	B	1 Ga SS Bttn			19 Sep 63	Was shot in the right breast, ball passing through body & coming out to the right of shoulder blade
John H. King	Life	D	15 Ga	Benning	Chickamauga	20 Sep 63	Was shot in the battle of Chickamauga, Ga. Minnie ball passing through left hip causing lameness
J. T. Glover, Jr.	Life	D	22 Ga	Wright	Virginia	23 Jun 63	Was shot in the bowels, ball passing

Record of Indigent Soldiers that Draw Pension from the State of Georgia in Jefferson County of 60 Dollars

The following transcription includes all of the listed information, combining the pensioner's time of service, amount of property, post office, and other extraneous notations, in the Notes column. All of the pensioners listed farmer as their occupation, except Wm Scarboro, who listed his occupation as nothing.

Name	Resident of Ga Since	Age	Co.	Regiment	Physical Condition	Notes
Bedgood, J.	1834	67	F	48 Ga	Health poor to general debility	Served 3½ years. No. property. Applied 1901. Bartow.
Covington, V. C.	1835	66	I	28 Ga	Ruptured & general debility.	Served 4 years. No property. Applied 1901. Avera.
Carroll, John	1834	67	F	10 Ga	Heart week & feeble	Served 3 years. No property. Applied 1901. Stellaville.
Dunaway, G. W.	1836	62	H	8 Ga Cav	General debility	Served 3 years. No property. Applied 1901. Avera.
Harden, C. W.	1840	70	F	8 Ga Cav	Rheumatism & general debility	Served 2½ years. No property. Applied 1901. Avera.
Howard, Thos.	1847	53	E	27 Ga Bttn	Piles &	Served 1 year. No

Name	Resident of Ga Since	Age	Co.	Regiment	Physical Condition	Notes
					rupture	property. Applied 1901. Wrens.
Smith, W^m						
Wary, W. F.	1833		G	38 Ga	Blindness & F[illegible]	Served 4 years. No property. Applied 1901. Louisville.
Irby, W. R.						Glascock County.
James, J. A.	1832	68	C	20 Ga	Rheumatism & rupture	Served 3½ years. No property. Applied 1901. Wrens.
Lafaver, Jno. T.	1840	59	I	28 Ga	Wounded in high & suffers with rheumatism & dropsy	Served 3 years. No property. Applied 1901. Avera.
King, T. G.	1843	58	B	55 Ga	Rupture & catarrh	Served 4 years. No property. Applied 1901. Avera.
Kitchens, Laurence	1834	67	B	22 Ga	Blindness	Served 4 years. No property. Applied 1901. Spread.
McGinnis, D. B.	1888	70	C	45 Ala	Wounded in both	Served 4 years. No

Name	Resident of Ga Since	Age	Co.	Regiment	Physical Condition	Notes
					shoulders.	property. Applied 1901. Davisboro.
Mullin, Jas. E.	1844	56		Howell Howard's Battery in Washington County	Bright's disease & rupture	Served 2⅓ years. Household furniture. Applied 1901. Grange.
Murphy, J. H.	1826	75	C	20 Ga	Very feeble, old age	Served 4 years. No property. Applied 1901. Avera.
Weeks, J. W.	1846	61	G	38 Ga	Shot through thigh & causes great pain	Served 3½ years. No property. Applied 1901. Noah.
Smith, W^m	1833	66	F	8 Ga Cav	Age & poverty	Served 2 years. No property. Applied 1901. Zebrina.
Newman, E, F.	1840	61	C	28 Ga	Shot in hip & leg broken	Served 4 years. No property. Applied 1901. Avera.
Pope, B. B.	1837	64	I	28 Ga	Heart trouble & infirm	Served 3½ years. No property. Applied 1901. Avera.

Name	Resident of Ga Since	Age	Co.	Regiment	Physical Condition	Notes
Pope, R. F.	1828	73	G	2 Ga	Old age & very feeble	Served 10 months. No property. Applied 1901. Avera. Transferred to Irwin County.
Page, Jos. Y.	1834	67	E	48 Ga	Blind	Served 3½ years. No property. Applied 1901. Wadley. Dead 1903.
Reese, M. E.	1836	75	H	48 Ga	Age & infirmity	Served 4 years. No property. Applied 1901. Avera.
Roberson, W						Drop.
Russell, John	1822	78	G	Ga Militia	Age & infirmity	Served 14 months. No property. Applied 1901. Wrens.
Sammons, H. L.	1837	63	B	22 Ga	Wounded in foot & hand. Was [illegible]	Served 4 years. $60. Applied 1901. Wrens.
Scarboro, W^{m}	1869	70	H	4	Wounded in breast, old age.	Served 3 years. Applied 1901. Bartow.
Screws, J. A.	1838	61	E	48 Ga	Eye right,	Served 4 years. No

Name	Resident of Ga Since	Age	Co.	Regiment	Physical Condition	Notes
					nearly blind.	property. Applied 1901. Bartow.
Stewart, A. A.	1830	71	F	8 Ga	Age & infirmity	Served 3 years. No property. Applied 1901. Wrens.
Swift, T. G.	1826	75	B I	48 Ga State Line	Blind & infirm	Served 10 months. No property. Applied 1901. Stapleton.
Stevens, W. L.						Louisville. Dead.
Stewart, J. B.	1834	67	G	38 Ga	Rheumatism & very feeble	Served 3 years. No property. Applied 1901. Wrens.
Underwood, Geo. F.	1834	66	F	8 Ga Cav	Blind & paralyzed	Served 3 years. No property. Applied 1901. Stapleton.
Whitehead, Robert	1815	85	Batty Guards	38 Ga	Age & infirmity	Served 1 year. No property. Applied 1901. Wrens.
Wilkinson, Jesse						Married to deceased.

Name	Resident of Ga Since	Age	Co.	Regiment	Physical Condition	Notes
Williams, J. L.	1826	75	I	28 Ga	Rheumatism & old age	Served 3 years. No property. Applied 1901. Avera.
Williams, R. E.	1839	62	I	28 Ga	Broken leg, disabled	Served 3½ years. No property. Applied 1901. Avera.
Peebles, J. L.	1840	60	D	12 Ga Bttn	Rheumatism, rupture & scull [illegible]	Served 3¼ years. No property. Applied 1900. Avera.
Easler, J. W.						Stapleton.
Nixon, Vernon	1827	74	I	28 Ga	Roten	Served 1 year. No property. Applied 1901. Louisville. Dead 1902.
March, John	1859	63	A	48 Ga	Wounded in wrist, not able from rheumatism	Served 2½ years. No property. Applied 1901. Davisboro.

List of Invalid Soldiers that draw Pensions from the State of Georgia that Reside in Jefferson County, Ga.

The following transcription combines the pensioner's place of service, when he drew a pension, the amount of the pension, and his post office in the Notes column.

Name	Co.	Regiment	Brigade	Wounded	Suffers Still	Notes
Becton, Curran	B	1 Bttn SS	Walker's	Right breast	With paralysis	Served in Georgia. Drew pension 1900. $50. Bartow.
Beall, S. S.	C	20 Ga	Benning's	In shoulder, in 1862	With said wound	Served in Virginia. Drew pension 1900. $50. Louisville.
Cain, J. G.						
Fields, W. J.	E	48 Ga	Wright's	In 1862, in right knee at Mechanicsville, Virginia	With said wound	Served in Virginia. First pension in 1901. $50. Bartow.
Ganus, E. J.	F	8 Ga Cav	Darian's	In 1864, in right side & lung	With said wound	Served in Virginia. Dead. Drew pension 1900. $50. Noah.
Glover, J. T.	B	22 Ga	Wright's	In 1863, bowels & hip, at Manassas Gap	With said wound	Served in Virginia. Drew pension 1900. $50. Spread.
Hinton, J. M.	F	10 Ga	Sims'	In 1863, right	With said	Served in Virginia.

71

Name	Co.	Regiment	Brigade	Wounded	Suffers Still	Notes
				shoulder	wound	Application approved 1901. $50. Matthews.
McGahee, J. M.	F	8 Ga Cav	Darian's	Horse falling near Greenville, North Carolina	With wound & rupture	Served in Virginia. Drew pension 1900. $50. Wrens.
Palmer, E.	E	Cobb's Legion		In 1864, fall from car, injured his head & convulsions up to present time	With epileptic fits	Served in Virginia. Drew pension 1900. $50. Moxley.
Phillips, W. H.	A	48 Ga	Wright's	1862, wound in right knee	Suffers with pain	Served in Virginia. Drew pension 1900. $50. [illegible]
Phillips, William	A	48 Ga	Wright's	1863, shot in breast	Cannot use left arm	Served in Virginia. Dead. Drew pension 1900. $50. Stellerville.
[faint], G. W.						Dead.
[faint], J. W.						Dead.
Rayburn, S. R.	A	48 Ga	Wright's	1862, shot in hand & snagged in bowels	Cannot use hand	Served in Virginia. Drew pension 1900. $25. Since increased to $50.

Name	Co.	Regiment	Brigade	Wounded	Suffers Still	Notes
						Stapleton.
Sanders, W^m	D	2 Ga	Benning's	1863, wounded in hip & finger shot off	Suffers still	Served in Virginia. Drew pension 1900. $50. Wrens.
Thomas, J. M.	L	Cobb's Legion	Hampton's	1863, shot in elbow	Suffer with stiffness & pain	Served Hagerstown, Maryland. Drew pension 1900. $50. Louisville. Dead.
Vause, W. A.	I	28 Ga	Colquitt's	1864, shot in leg	Caused amputation	Served in Virginia. Drew pension 1900. $100. Avera.
Walden, W. G.	C	20 Ga	Benning's	1862, shot in left groin	Unable to work	Served in Virginia. Drew pension 1900. $50. Avera.
Wiggins, E. M.	B	59 Ga	Anderson's			Served in Virginia. Drew pension 1900. $50. Moxley.
Wood, J. A.	B	22 Ga	Wright's	Shot through thigh & hip	With discharge of pus	Served in Virginia. Drew pension 1900. $50.

Name	Co.	Regiment	Brigade	Wounded	Suffers Still	Notes
						Spread.
Young, C. W.	H	63 Ga	Mercer's	1864, shot in foot	With lameness	Kennesaw Mountain. Drew pension 1900. $25. Wrens. Now applicant awaiting to be approved Sep 1903. [Last note in left lower margin of page. Difficult to know whether not refers to this soldier, one of the next three soldiers, or all four soldiers.]
McDaniel, L. B.	E	48 Ga	Wright's	1862	Suffers still, cannot work	Second Manassas. Applied 1901. Moxley. Disapproved.
McNeely, Thos. M.	E	48 Ga	Wright's		Cannot work	Gettysburg. Moxley. Disapproved.
Jones, J. W.	E	48 Ga	Wright's	1863 & captured, remained a prisoner until Feb 1865, then paroled	Old & suffer from wound	Manassas Gap, 22 Jul 1863. Applied 1901. Bartley.

Name	Co.	Regiment	Brigade	Wounded	Suffers Still	Notes
						Disapproved.
Walters, G. W.						Disapproved.

Applicants for Pensions of (Indigent Class) of Soldiers in the Civil War Sent to the Commission for Approval Sept 1st 1901

The following transcription combines the date and place of birth into one column and the pensioner's date and place of enlistment, length of service, where surrendered or discharged, and post office, as well as any extraneous notations made by the clerk, in the Notes column.

Name	How long in Ga	Birth	Co.	Regiment	Notes
Arington, Silas A.	All his life	19 Jun 1836, Jefferson County	B	59 Ga	Enlisted 1862. Surrendered Appomattox, 1865. Stapleton.
Barrow, Henry	Since 1822	1812, Green County, North Carolina	G	2 Ga	Enlisted 1862, Jefferson County. Surrendered Apr 1865, Honey Hill, South Carolina. Dead. Matthews.
Bedingfield, H. J.	All his life	24 Jan 1838, Jefferson County	E	48 Ga	Enlisted 4 Mar 1862, Jefferson County. Was not present at surrender, at home on furlough sick. Wadley. Disapproved.
Cowart, S. L.	All his life	1 Oct 1824, Jefferson County	L	Cobb's Legion	Enlisted 1862, Jefferson County. Served until Apr 1862. Old age & disability. Vines.
Dixon, W. R.	All his life	10 May 1838 Burke County	C	32 Ga	Enlisted 12 May 1862, Burke County. Served 3 years until surrender Apr 1865. Matthews. Dead.

Name	How long in Ga	Birth	Co.	Regiment	Notes
					Disapproved.
Fleming, Samuel P.	All his life	22 Apr 1835, Jefferson County	F	Cobb's Legion	Enlisted May 1862. Served until surrender Apr 1865, Greensboro, North Carolina. Wrens. Disapproved.
Fleming, Wm W.	All his life	2 Feb 1825, Jefferson County	L	Cobb's Legion	Enlisted Nov 1862, Jefferson County. Served 3 years until surrender Apr 1865, Greensboro, North Carolina. Vines. Disapproved.
Gordon, James	All his life	7 May 1828, Burke County	F	Cobb's Legion	Enlisted Mar 1862. Served until Johnson's surrender, Apr 1865, Greensboro, North Carolina. Louisville. Dead.
Kendrick, Geo. W.	All his life	12 Dec 1836, Columbia County	E	48 Ga	Enlisted Mar 1862 in Louisville. Served until surrender Apr 1865, Appomattox. Noah.
Moxley, W. D.	All his life	Mar 1839, Burke County	E	48 Ga	Enlisted 10 Mar 1862, Louisville. Served until surrender 9 Apr 1865, Appomattox. Moxley. Disapproved.

Name	How long in Ga	Birth	Co.	Regiment	Notes
Marsh, John	All his life	1841, Glascock County	A	48 Ga	Enlisted May 1862. Transferred to Co. I, 48 Ga, 1864. Served until surrender with General Lee. Grange.
Matthews, Moses F.	All his life	6 Jul 1846, Warren County	I	28 Ga Militia	Enlisted May 1864. Served 11 months until surrender Apr 1865, Augusta. Wrens. Disapproved.
Landrum, P. H.	All his life	1841, Warren County	A	27 Ga	Enlisted Apr 1863. Served until surrender Apr 1865, Greensboro, North Carolina. Wrens.
McNeely, Denny	All his life	1817, Jefferson County	A		Enlisted 1863. At Decatur & then detached & put [illegible]. Served until surrender. "*I was in Macon, Ga. Guarding Prisoners when my Co. Surrendered.*" After Sherman's army passed, guarding prisoners. Louisville. Disapproved.
McNair, S. J.	All his life	1831, Columbia County	E	48 Ga	Enlisted 1862. Served 4 years until surrender, 1865, Appomattox.

Name	How long in Ga	Birth	Co.	Regiment	Notes
					Dead. Sandy.
Roberts, J. W.	Since 1851	1845, Orangeburg County, South Carolina	B	27 Ga Bttn	Enlisted Sep 1863, Augusta. Served 1½ years. In Augusta hospital at surrender. Louisville. Disapproved.
Saxon, Ransom	All his life	1836, Burke County	A	3 Ga	Enlisted 1861, Augusta. Served until 2 days before the surrender, 1865, Appomattox. Taken prisoner, Farmville, Virginia & carried to Point Lookout.
Thompson, W. R.	All his life	30 Aug 1840, Jefferson County	F	8 Ga Cav	Enlisted Jun 1862. Served 11 months, furnished substitute & then joined militia, nearly 2 years in Georgia. The entire militia discharged 15 Feb 1865 in Augusta. Avera. Disapproved
Williams, Simeon A.	All his life	Oct 1837, Jefferson County	I	28 Ga	Enlisted Mar 1862. Served until surrender Apr 1865, Greensboro, North Carolina. Was in hospital at surrender. Spread.
Wimberly, Homer	All his	Oct 1833,	C	32 Ga	Enlisted may 1862. Served until

Name	How long in Ga	Birth	Co.	Regiment	Notes
	life	Burke County			surrender Apr 1865, Augusta. Louisville.
Williams, J. F.	All his life	1831, Jefferson County	I	28 Ga	Enlisted Mar 1862. Served until close of war Mar 1865 at Point Lookout. Rupture & disability. Spread. Dead.
Turner, Thos.	All his life	1832, Hancock County	A	48 Ga	Enlisted 1862. Served 4 months until surrender 1865. Was on government steamer at close of war. Louisville.
Hatcher, Robert	Since 1850	1836, Edgefield, South Carolina	B	19 SC	Enlisted 1862 Columbia, South Carolina. Served 3 years. No present at surrender, sick. Louisville. Approved 1902.
Ivery, G. H. L.	Since 26 Sep 1826	1826, Elbert County	A	7 Cav	Enlisted 1862. Served 3 years. Approved 1902.
Paradise, W. D.	Since Dec 1833	1833, Jefferson County	G	57 Ga	Enlisted 1862. Served 3¼ years. Approved 1902.
Page, W. H.	All his life	1835, Emmanuel County	B	20 Ga	Enlisted 1862. Served 3 years. Approved 1902.
Willeford, H. P.	All his	1833, Jefferson	B	22 Ga	Enlisted 1862. Served 3½ years.

Name	How long in Ga	Birth	Co.	Regiment	Notes
	life	County			Approved 1903.
Beasley, A.		1825	G	1 Ga	Enlisted 1863. Served 2 years. Approved 1903.

Muster Roll of Captain James Stapleton's Company

The muster roll is typewritten.

Muster Roll of Captain James Stapleton's Company (H) of the 12 Georgia Regiment of Cavalry, Army of the Confederate States of America, (Colonel H. G. Wright,) from the 6th day of January 1864, when last mustered, to the __ day of __, 186_.

No.	Name	Rank	Enlisted	By Whom
1	James Stapleton	Captain	Louisville	A. J. Holmes for 6 months
2	Willis Howard	1st Lieutenant	4 Aug, Louisville	A. J. Holmes for 6 months
3	L. D. Matthews	2nd Sr. Lieutenant		
4	Abram Beesley	2 Jr. Lieutenant		
1	E. A. Sikes	1st Sergeant		
2	J. M. Codowns	2 Sergeant		
3	A. J. Holmes	3rd Sergeant		
4	~~J. P. Stapleton~~			
5	R. L. Terrell	X Sergeant		
1	William Clark	1 Corporal		
2	W. W. Stapleton	2nd Corporal		
3	John Russell	3rd Corporal		
4	G. C. Gaynus	4th Corporal		
1	Analey, H. T.	Private		
2	Adams, John	Private		
3	~~Clark, J. W.~~	Private		
4	Daniel, J. P.	Private		
5	Dickson, Samuel	Private		

No.	Name	Rank	Enlisted	By Whom
6	Freeman, G. A.	Private		
7	Farmer, J. J.	Private		
8	Ford, James	Private		
9	~~Gaynus, William~~	Private		
10	Hudson, J. C.	Private		
11	Hatcher, Rufus	Private		
12	Hadden, R. J. C.	Private		
13	Johnson, R. S.	Private		
14	Kendrick, M. P.	Private		
15	Lucky, Abraham	Private		
16	Lafever, Allen	Private		
17	Mercer, R. A.	Private		
18	McNair, G. F.	Private		
19	Oliphant, W. J.	Private		
20	Pope, B. B.	Private		
21	Philip, James	Private		
22	Perdue, Jackson	Private	No marker, buried	family grave
23	Perdue, William	Private	Near Mt. Horam.	Son John at Kite.
24	Parker, S. D.	Private		
25	Philip, William	Private		
26	Philip, Willis	Private		
27	Russell, Charles	Private		
28	Swan, William	Private		

No.	Name	Rank	Enlisted	By Whom
29	Smith, William	Private		
30	Trimble, J. L.	Private		
31	Thompson, W. S.	Private		
32	Thompson, J. M.	Private		
33	Thompson, S. R.	Private		
34	Wren, J. J.	Private		
35	Wren, Jeptha	Private		
36	Wren, J. P.	Private		
37	Williams, J. M.	Private		
38	Washington, G. T.	Private		
39	Whitaker, J. E.	Private		21 Jan Camp Wright
40	Whitaker, J. P.	Private		
41	Stepleton, J. D.	Private		
42	Clark, J. W.	Private		
43	Gaynos, William	Private		
44	Thompson, J. M.	Private		
45	Lou, James E.	Private		
46	Lamp, William A.	Private		

List of Approved Applications of Soldiers & Widows From 1920 To ___

The list apparently includes the names of widows whose pension applications were approved after 1920, not necessarily all of those receiving pensions after 1920. The third column is the date of enlistment.

Name	Husband	Enl.	Co.	Regiment	Marriage
Susan F. Drane 1928	Wm. W.	15 Apr 1861	H	2 Ala. Inf.	6 Nov 1867
Rilla M. Eve 1928 (2)	McP. Ber.	20 May 1861		Major on staff of Gen. H. C. Wayne	16 Oct 1866
Catherine McGraw 1926 (3)	Henry C.	About Jul or Aug 1864	No Co.	No Regt. Given	Dec 1870
Emma Oxford 1925	William	10 May 1862		Howell's Battery	10 Feb 1880
Savannah Perdue 1910	Ben. N.	4 Mar 1862	E	48 Ga. Inf.	20 Aug 1868
Cornelia Peebles Thompson 1930	Thos. J.	1 Oct 1861	G	38 Ga. Inf.	About 1868
Caroline Williams 1902	J. N.	1 Jul 1862	F	8 Ga. Cav.	15 Jan 1860

State of Georgia
Pension Department
Atlanta

R. deT. Lawrence
Commissioner of Pensions

January 29, 1931

Hon. Louisa M. Wright
Ordinary of Jefferson County
Louisville, Ga.

My dear Judge:

On a separate sheet I am sending you the information requested in your letter of January 27.

Mrs. McGraw furnishes no company and regiment in which her husband, Henry C. McGraw served. She states, however, that her first husband, Franklin Hadden, died in a hospital in Mississippi in 1863. Since we are not able to check out the record of Henry C. McGraw, will you not make inquiry of Mrs. McGraw as to the first husband's company and regiment so that her claim may be strengthened by adding the record of the first husband.

With kind regards,

Very truly yours,

R. deT. Lawrence

Louisville, Georgia
January 19th 1931

Hon. H. L. Thomas
Ordinary Telfair County
McRae, Georgia

In Re: Transferring Mrs. Texas E. Nash from Pension Roll of Telfair o Jefferson

Dear Judge:

Mrs. Texas E. Nash wished to be transferred from Telfair Pension Roll to Jefferson County. I am attaching her request hereto.

I expect you had better make the transfer for the February Pay Roll as I have made up the January Pay Roll for 1931.

With kind regards, I am
Very truly yours,

Louisa M. Wright, Ordinary
Jeff. Co. Ga.

Judge H. M. Thomas
Ordinary Telfair County
McRae, Georgia

Dear Judge Thomas:

Please transfer me from your County Pension Roll to Jefferson County Pension Roll, as soon as possible. I am living in Jefferson County now with one of my daughters.

With kind regards and many thanks for your kindness to me, I am

Very truly yours,

Mrs. Texas E. Nash

State of Georgia, Telfair County

I H. L. Thomas Ordinary of said County Do Hereby Transfer The Above Pensioner From Telfair County Pay Roll to Jefferson County Pay Roll To Begin In February 1931. So I Will Leave Her Off My Roll and To Be Placed On The Roll Of Jefferson County. H. L. Thomas, Ordinary.

Filed in Office Jan. 27, 1931. Louisa M. Wright, Ordinary

State of Georgia
Pension Department
Atlanta

May 31, 1930

Hon. Louisa M. Wright
Ordinary of Jefferson County

Louisville, Ga.

My dear Judge:

A reply to your letter of May 20, has been delayed on account of our inability to get to our records. For a week or more we have been seriously handicapped by repair work in the Capitol and for two days had o abandon our offices entirely.

We have been able to get the information you wish today, however, and give it below as follows:

Mrs. Emma Oxford, widow of William Oxford, married Feb. 10, 1880.

Mrs. Judia Russell, Enrolled Jefferson County, 1910. Widow of Charles Russell, Co. H., 12th Ga. Inf. Married in Jefferson Co., Apr. 23, 1857.

Mrs. Matie N. Simmons, widow of John A. Simmons, Co. I, 59th Ga. Married Jan. 30, 1868. Enrolled Jefferson Co., 1910.

With kind regards,

R. deT. Lawrence
Commissioner of Pensions

COPY

State of Georgia
Pension Department
Atlanta

Ho. Louisa M. Wright
Ordinary of Jefferson County
Louisville, Ga.

My dear Judge:

Your letter of May 17, requesting the record of Captain William Alexander Willie, whose widow, Mrs. Annie H. Willie is on the pension roll of Georgia, has been received.

There is no witness to this application but I quote as follows from a letter from the War Department attached to the application which gives the official record of William A. Willie in Co. D, 1st Regiment Florida Infantry, C. S. A.:

> "The records show that William A. Willie served as a sergeant of Companies D and I, 1st Regiment Florida Inf., C. S. A., and as sergeant major of the Field and Staff of he 1st Regiment Florida Inf., C. S. A., and that he was discharged with the rank of sergeant major March 29, 1862, by reason of the expiration of his term of service. The certificate of his eligibility for discharge is dated Montgomery, Ala., March 29, 1862, and is signed by H. H. Baker, Sr., Captain, commanding Company E, (1st) Florida Regiment."

With kind regards,

Very truly yours,

R. deT. Lawrence

Jefferson Approved

Mrs. A. G. Powell, widow of A. G. Powell, Co. E, 48 Ga, husband on roll.

Mrs. Mattie Farmer, widow of Rhesa E. Farmer, Co. B, 27th Bttn, husband on roll.

Mrs. Miner Gunn, widow of Lewis F. Gunn, husband on roll.

Mrs. Mary J. Bedingfield, widow of N. W. Bedingfield, husband on roll.

State of Georgia
Pension Department
Atlanta

March 4th 1925

Jefferson County,

A. G. Lafavor

DISAPPROVED, because I regret my inability to find in this application or the official record proof of service to the end of the War. (DISAPPROVED, also in 1920.)

Henry McGraw

DISAPPROVED, for the reason that applicant is not shown to have served for six months as required by law, and applicant and witness not with their commands at end of the War.

N. E. Harris
Commissioner of Pensions

Approved Widows for 1920 Jefferson County

The last column includes the date the widow married the veteran and the name of the witness who testified that the marriage took place. The words license and record may indicate that the marriage took place in Jefferson County and the record was on file in the Ordinary's office.

Name	Widow of	Co.	Regiment	Marriage & Witness
Averett, Sallie F.	E. M.	D	12 Ga. Militia	72- J. W. Haddock
Aldred, W. N.	W. N.	I	5 Ga. Inf.	12 May 76 W. H. English & license
Bell, Josephine	Green J.	G	57 Ga. Inf.	1876 – J. C. King & license
Brown, Julia M.	Burrell J.	B	27 Ga. Bttn.	18 Nov 63 – John J. Whigham & his record
Brown, E. L.	Aua	K	48 Ga. Inf.	5 Dec 77 – A. G. Powell & record
Dawson, Eliza	J. B.	F	Cobb's Legion	15 Jul 78 – J. M. Kennedy & license
Denny, J. K.	J. K.	B	27 Ga. Bttn.	10 Dec 76 – R. H. Farmer & record
Farmer, Adeline	L. D.	B	27 Ga. Bttn.	1864 – R. F. Farmer & record
Hutto, L. B.	L. B.			6 Feb 63 – Husband on roll
Hopkins, A. N. B.	M. H.	I	1 Vol. Inf.	18 Sep 67 – J. H. Polhill
Hauser, L. C.	W. C.	F	Cobb's Legion	11 Nov 69 – J. M. Kennedy & license
Harmon, N. T.	N. T.	F	8th Confederate Cavalry	Aug 1862 – J. C. Harmon

Name	Widow of	Co.	Regiment	Marriage & Witness
Irby, Jane	A. J.	I	28 Ga. Inf.	1 Jul 77 – K. J. Harvey & record
Johnson, S. A.	G. G.	F	Cobb's Legion	27 Apr 76 – J. M. Kennedy & record
McMillan, Hattie	Jno. A.	B	20 Ga. Cav.	21 Oct 73 – Wm Calhoun & license - record
McKay, G. A.	E. D.	C	20 Ga. Inf.	29 Jan 1873 – B. J. Moxley & record
Nash, Texas E.	H. A.	C	4 Ga. Inf.	3 Oct 80 – Jno. Clance & record.
Perdue, Martha A.	A. M.	C	20 Ga. Inf.	Dec 1870 – H. B. Young
Pate, N. G.	N. G.	I	5 Ga. Militia	6 Feb 72 – W. E. English
Raines, Lou	J. B.	D	27 Ga. Bttn.	12 Mar 79 – J. L. Rains
Sammons, Mary	A. H.	B	22 Ga. Inf.	Oct 66 – T. R. Railey – license & record
Wilson, M. J.	J. T.	B	22 Ga. Inf.	16 Sep 65 – T. R. Railey & record
Denny, W. A.	W. A.	B	27 Ga. Bttn.	11 Dec 79 – R. K. Farmer & record

Approved Soldiers for 1920, Jefferson County

The witness likely verified the veteran's military service. The meaning of the word record is unclear.

Name	Co.	Regiment	Witness
Barton, W. E.	K	16 Ga. Inf.	A. J. Avery & record
Bedingfield, N. W.	E	48 Ga. Inf.	A. G. Pound & record
Denton, David	I	28 Ga. Inf.	J. M. Varner
Everetts, J. B.	C	26 Ga. Inf.	J. M. Ruskin
Farmer, R. E.	B	27 Ga. Bttn.	J. J. Whigham
Harvey, H. J.	I	28 Ga. Inf.	H. F. Newman & record
Haden, S. T.	F	8 Ga. Cav.	S. F. Beasley
Pennington, M.	G	6 Ga. Res.	Wm. E. Keener
Powell, A. C.	K	48 Ga. Inf.	N. W. Bedingfield
Polhill, J. H.	C	20 Ga. Inf.	Record, A. T. Lender
Rabun, H. A.	G	27 Ga. Inf.	W. H. Luckey
Thigpen, A. J.	I	28 Ga. Inf.	M. I. Harvey & record
Smith, A. S.	G	38 Ga. Inf.	L. I. Stewart
Rhodes, J. H.	D	1 Ga Vol. Inf.	Record

To Confederate Veterans, Their Widows, Sons and Daughters

The following published handbill from the Commissioner of Pensions is self explanatory.

April 22, 1924

By C. E. McGregor
Commissioner of Pensions
State Capitol
Atlanta

Notwithstanding the law DEMANDS that the pensioners of the State shall be paid their pensions between January and May each year, not since 1910 has that law been complied with.

For some cause, the State was divided into two sections and the pensioners living in one section were paid in the Spring and those in the other section paid in the Fall.

Why?

Don't ask me. Ask the other fellows.

The average age of the veterans in the Confederate Soldiers' Home being over eighty-one years, I think it safe to assume that the average age of the pensioners on the pension rolls is not less than seventy-nine years. To delay paying what was due in January, for six months, means that nearly twelve per cent of the pension money would be handled by the undertakers and grave-diggers and not by the pensioners. Therefore, I notified the Governor that I expected to comply with the law and pay all the pensioners their pensions for 1924 between January and May. He assured me that he would heartily co-operate, and, if the tax money was not in the Treasury, he would exhaust the borrowing power of the State to accomplish it. On the 18th day of April he notified me that I could arrange to pay all the pensioners in the State a pension of $100.00 by the 26th day of April.

Anticipating the Governor's assent, the clerical force of the Pension Department was ready for immediate action, and, while I write, the State Treasurer is preparing checks to send to the County Ordinaries, so that every pensioner can receive the pension not later than April 30th.

A word of explanation about the "old" and "new" classes of pensioners. Up to, and including, 1919, the possession of $1,500.00 in money or property excluded a veteran from having his name put upon the official Honor Roll – the pension list. The sons and grand-sons and the daughters and grand-daughters of the Confederate heroes rebelled against the unjust discrimination and formulated a Constitutional amendment wiping out the obnoxious inhibition and COMMANDING that future legislatures SHALL provide by taxation for their pensions.

95

Said amendment was adopted by the General Assembly and ratified by the people at the general election in 1920.

The General Assembly appropriated sufficient funds to pay those newly admitted members of the pension rolls for the years 1920 and 1921, and they were paid in full. To pay this same class of pensioners for 1922 and 1923, the General Assembly again appropriated the full amount allowed by the statute. Thos. W. Hardwick, the then Governor, vetoed this appropriation. The then acting Commissioner of Pensions – an appointee of Hardwick's – quietly acquiesced in this most monstrously autocratic and anarchistic usurpation of executive power ever attempted in Georgia, and the veterans and widows of veterans, known as the "new" class, who had been admitted to the Pension Rolls by an amendment to the State Constitution, were burglarized out of their pensions for 1922 and 1923. That's one thing the "do something Governor" did, which largely contributed to his defeat in the next general election. Another thing this "do something Governor" did was to withhold his veto from the records of your State. It was only after the present Commissioner of Pensions was installed in office, and only after an exhaustive and diligent effort on his part, that said veto was unearthed and admitted to record, July 10th, 1923. The veto was issued August 21, 1922, eleven months prior to its being recorded.

Will these "new" class of pensioners of 1922 and 1923, who were robbed of their pensions for those years by T. W. Hardwick, ever be paid? If the cigar and cigarette tax is sustained by the courts and enforced, and your Commissioner of Pensions will place the pensioners above politics, YES!

Respectfully submitted,

C. E. McGregor
Commissioner of Pensions

Miscellaneous Correspondence and Other Loose Papers

The following transcriptions include a variety of correspondence mostly to or from the Jefferson County Ordinary, as well as other loose papers, concerning various Confederate pensioners and the pension program.

Louisville, Georgia
April 14th 1951

Hon. Carl Vinson
House of Representatives
Washington, D. C.

In Re: Confederate War record of Wm. A. Willie, Sgt., Co. D, 1st Regiment Fla. Inf., C. S. A.

Dear Mr. Vinson:

Mrs. Nora Willie Godbee, Louisville, Ga., wants to know when her father, the above named Confederate Veteran enlisted, and any other information you can give of his service. She wishes it to fill out her application for "The Cross of Iron", the U. D. C's. give to descendants of the veterans.

Very truly yours,

_____, Ordinary
Jeff. Co., Ga.

Jefferson has Eight New Pensioners That Have Qualified Under The New Act, Known As Class B.

Under the new law, allowing widows of Confederate Soldiers that were married before 1920 to their Soldier Husbands and have not remarried since, Eight Widows have qualified and are now drawing their Pensions. Viz.

Mrs. Lizzie Atwell, Wrens,

Mrs. Belle Culver, Bartow,

Mrs. Susan Dickey, Bartow,

Mrs. Lella Kendrick, Wrens,

Mrs. Nellie P. Little, Louisville,

Mrs. Mary Moxley, Wadley,

Mrs. Mollie Reese, Avera,

Mrs. Susie Reeves, Wrens.

State Department of Public Welfare
Hurt Building
Atlanta

Miss Louisa M. Wright, Ordinary
Jefferson County
Louisville, Ga.

WHEREAS:

MRS. LIZZIE ATWELL, WIDOW OF JAMES ATWELL,

Has filed in this office an application for the Georgia pension allowed to widows of Confederate veterans; and it appearing that the late husband of his applicant performed actual military service as a Confederate soldier and was honorably separated from such service; and that applicant was married to said soldier prior to January 1st, 1920, and that she was nor remarried; it is, therefore,

ORDERED:

That said applicant be admitted to the pension roll of the State of Georgia for the month of January, 1936, and thereafter; and that a copy of this order be sent to the Ordinary of said County.

This, the 27th day of December 1937.

L. Thos. "Pat" Fillen
Director, Confederate Division

State Department of Public Welfare
Hurt Building
Atlanta

Miss Louisa M. Wright, Ordinary
Jefferson County
Louisville, Ga.

WHEREAS:

MRS. BELLE T. CULVER, WIDOW OF BEN C. CULVER,

Has filed in this office an application for the Georgia pension allowed to widows of Confederate veterans; and it appearing that the late husband of his applicant performed actual military service as a Confederate soldier and was honorably separated from such service; and that applicant was married to said soldier prior to January 1st, 1920, and that she was nor remarried; it is, therefore,

ORDERED:

That said applicant be admitted to the pension roll of the State of Georgia for the month of January, 1936, and thereafter; and that a copy of this order be sent to the Ordinary of said County.

This, the 27th day of December 1937.

L. Thos. "Pat" Fillen
Director, Confederate Division

State Department of Public Welfare
Hurt Building
Atlanta

Miss Louisa M. Wright, Ordinary
Jefferson County
Louisville, Ga.

WHEREAS:

MRS. SUSAN A. DICKEY, WIDOW OF W. H. DICKEY,

Has filed in this office an application for the Georgia pension allowed to widows of Confederate veterans; and it appearing that the late husband of his applicant performed actual military service as a Confederate soldier and was honorably separated from such service; and that applicant was married to said soldier prior to January 1st, 1920, and that she was nor remarried; it is, therefore,

ORDERED:

That said applicant be admitted to the pension roll of the State of Georgia for the month of January, 1936, and thereafter; and that a copy of this order be sent to the Ordinary of said County.

This, the 27th day of December 1937.

L. Thos. "Pat" Fillen
Director, Confederate Division

State Department of Public Welfare
Hurt Building
Atlanta

Miss Louisa M. Wright, Ordinary
Jefferson County
Louisville, Ga.

WHEREAS:

MRS. LELA KENDRICK, WIDOW OF JOHN PAYBON KENDRICK,

Has filed in this office an application for the Georgia pension allowed to widows of Confederate veterans; and it appearing that the late husband of his applicant performed actual military service as a Confederate soldier and was honorably separated from such service; and that applicant was married to said soldier prior to January 1st, 1920, and that she was nor remarried; it is, therefore,

ORDERED:

That said applicant be admitted to the pension roll of the State of Georgia for the month of January, 1936, and thereafter; and that a copy of this order be sent to the Ordinary of said County.

This, the 27th day of December 1937.

L. Thos. "Pat" Fillen
Director, Confederate Division

State Department of Public Welfare
Hurt Building
Atlanta

Miss Louisa M. Wright, Ordinary
Jefferson County
Louisville, Ga.

WHEREAS:

MRS. NELLIE P. LITTLE, WIDOW OF J. C. LITTLE,

Has filed in this office an application for the Georgia pension allowed to widows of Confederate veterans; and it appearing that the late husband of his applicant performed actual military service as a Confederate soldier and was honorably separated from such service; and that applicant was married to said soldier prior to January 1st, 1920, and that she was nor remarried; it is, therefore,

ORDERED:

That said applicant be admitted to the pension roll of the State of Georgia for the month of January, 1936, and thereafter; and that a copy of this order be sent to the Ordinary of said County.

This, the 27th day of December 1937.

L. Thos. "Pat" Fillen
Director, Confederate Division

State Department of Public Welfare
Hurt Building
Atlanta

State Department of Public Welfare
Hurt Building
Atlanta

Miss Louisa M. Wright, Ordinary
Jefferson County
Louisville, Ga.

WHEREAS:

MRS. MARY E. MOXLEY, WIDOW OF WM. D. MOXLEY,

Has filed in this office an application for the Georgia pension allowed to widows of Confederate veterans; and it appearing that the late husband of his applicant performed actual military service as a Confederate soldier and was honorably separated from such service; and that applicant was married to said soldier prior to January 1st, 1920, and that she was nor remarried; it is, therefore,

ORDERED:

That said applicant be admitted to the pension roll of the State of Georgia for the month of January, 1936, and thereafter; and that a copy of this order be sent to the Ordinary of said County.

This, the 27th day of December 1937.

L. Thos. "Pat" Fillen
Director, Confederate Division

State Department of Public Welfare
Hurt Building
Atlanta

Miss Louisa M. Wright, Ordinary
Jefferson County
Louisville, Ga.

WHEREAS:

MRS. MOLLIE REESE, WIDOW OF M. E. REESE,

Has filed in this office an application for the Georgia pension allowed to widows of Confederate veterans; and it appearing that the late husband of his applicant performed actual military service as a Confederate soldier and was honorably separated from such service; and that applicant was married to said soldier prior to January 1st, 1920, and that she was nor remarried; it is, therefore,

ORDERED:

That said applicant be admitted to the pension roll of the State of Georgia for the month of January, 1936, and thereafter; and that a copy of this order be sent to the Ordinary of said County.

This, the 27th day of December 1937.

L. Thos. "Pat" Fillen
Director, Confederate Division

State Department of Public Welfare
Hurt Building
Atlanta

Miss Louisa M. Wright, Ordinary
Jefferson County
Louisville, Ga.

WHEREAS:

MRS. SUSIE REEVES, WIDOW OF CHARLES REEVES,

Has filed in this office an application for the Georgia pension allowed to widows of Confederate veterans; and it appearing that the late husband of his applicant performed actual military service as a Confederate soldier and was honorably separated from such service; and that applicant was married to said soldier prior to January 1st, 1920, and that she was nor remarried; it is, therefore,

ORDERED:

That said applicant be admitted to the pension roll of the State of Georgia for the month of January, 1936, and thereafter; and that a copy of this order be sent to the Ordinary of said County.

This, the 27th day of December 1937.

L. Thos. "Pat" Fillen
Director, Confederate Division

State of Georgia
Pension Department
Atlanta

November 24, 1925

Hon. Jas. F. Brown
Louisville, Ga.

Dear Judge:

In reply to your letter of recent date wish to say that the names of Mrs. Mollie Reeves (now Pool) and Mrs. Sallie F. Averett (Mrs. O. H. P. Beall) have been placed on roll for the back pay, Mrs. Reeves to receive $225.00, and Mrs. Averett $150.00.

Very truly yours,

John W. Clark
Commissioner of Pensions

November 13, 1925

Hon. Jas. F. Brown
Louisville, Ga.

Dear Judge:

The application of Mrs. Emma Oxford, widow of Wm. Oxford, Deceased Pensioner, has been approved by me. You may place her name on your roll for 1926 payment.

Very truly yours,

John W. Clark
Commissioner of Pensions

State of Georgia
Pension Department
Atlanta

September 26, 1925

Hon. J. F. Brown
Ordinary of Jefferson County
Louisville, Georgia

Dear Judge:

In your letter of the 22, instant you ask this question: "Does this mean all in life then or all in life now?" It means the living only as we understand it.

Replying to your inquiry in regard to Mrs. Reeves: Yes, Mrs. Reeves is entitled to the amount that was due her, or rather the balance of the amount that was due her ~~before she remarried~~.

We regret the blanks have not reached you promptly, however, we are sending you by today's mail more of them and hope you will receive them on time, if not, notify us and we will forward more at once.

Very truly yours,

John W. Clark
Commissioner of Pensions

State of Georgia
Pension Department
Atlanta

September 30, 1925

Hon. Jas. F. Brown
Ordinary of Jefferson County
Louisville, Georgia

Dear Judge:

Replying to your letter of the 28 instant, beg to inform you that the back pensions are for the living only. These have been our instructions and according to them the widow will not draw her soldier husband's back pension.

Very truly yours,

John W. Clark
Commissioner of Pensions

Millin, Ga.
March 28th 1925

Mr. Brown,

Dear Sir,

Mr. Oxford is dead. He ask me to write you and ask you to Please send his Papers to me and for me to sign them like he sign them so I could so I could get his mony to pay his Burring Expenses. That is all he talk about. He wanted to live to get his Pension so bad to bury him. He had me to write you last week he was on his way home when he was taken sick. He said he believe you would do that for him. I am not able to pay it for I have nothing to pay with. Mr. Brown please do that for him for I do want his Buring Expenses and Dr. bill paid. He said to write you and tell you please do that for him. Please let me know if you will do that.

Yours respectfully,

Mrs. Emma Oxford
38 Krauss Ave.
Millen, Ga.

Ans by post card Mch 30, 1925

State of Georgia
Pension Department
Atlanta

July 26, 1926

Hon. Jas. F. Brown
Ordinary of Jefferson County
Louisville, Georgia

Dear Judge:

The application of Thomas S. Moore has been approved and you may place his name on your
roll for the Third Quarterly Payment.

Very truly yours,

John W. Clark
Commissioner of Pensions

State of Georgia
Pension Department
Atlanta

September 27, 1928

Hon. Louisa M. Wright
Ordinary of Jefferson County
Louisville, Ga.

Dear dear Judge:

Your letter of September 26, requesting the company and regiment of Thomas S. Moore, has been received.

I find this soldier was enrolled as a member of Co. K, 28th Georgia and Co. C, 54th Georgia.

Very truly yours,

John W. Clark
Commissioner of Pensions
By Margaret W. Arnold, Clerk

State of Georgia
Pension Department
Atlanta

July 18, 1927

Hon. Louisa Wright
Ordinary of Jefferson County
Louisville, Ga.

Dear dear Judge:

The application of Mr. J. T. Myers has been disapproved for the reason that there is not sufficient military service.

With kind regards,

Very truly yours,

John W. Clark
Commissioner of Pensions

State of Georgia
Pension Department
Atlanta

May 11, 1928

Hon. Louisa M. Wright
Ordinary of Jefferson County
Louisville, Georgia

Dear dear Judge:

It is my pleasure to inform you that the application of Mrs. Rilla M. Eve to become enrolled a pensioner as the widow of McPherson B. Eve, Major on the staff of General H. C. Wayne during the War Between the States, has been approved and you may place her name on your roll to receive the Second Quarter payment.

With kind regards,

Yours very truly,

John W. Clark
Commissioner of Pensions

P. S. The name of Mrs. Eve has been added to your Second Quarter roll which I note has already been received in this office. J. W. C.

State of Georgia
Pension Department
Atlanta

October 8, 1928

Hon. Louisa M. Wright
Ordinary of Jefferson County
Louisville, Georgia.

Dear dear Judge:

The application of Mrs. Ellen T. Moore to be enrolled a pensioner in her own right as the widow of Thomas S. Moore, member of Companies "K" 28th, and "C" 54th Georgia Regiments, Confederate States Army, has been approved and you may add her name to your roll to receive the Fourth Quarter payment.

With kind regards,

Very truly yours,

John W. Clark
Commissioner of Pensions
By Margaret W. Arnold, Clerk

State of Georgia
Pension Department
Atlanta

November 16, 1928

Hon. Louisa M. Wright
Ordinary of Jefferson County
Louisville, Georgia.

Dear dear Judge:

The application of Mrs. Mollie Barrow to be enrolled a pensioner in her own right as the widow of Henry Barrow, member of Company "C" 2nd Georgia Militia, Confederate States Army, has been approved and her name added to your Fourth Quarter roll to receive this payment.

This is your authority to pay to her the fifty dollars which will be included in your check when the payment is made.

With kind regards,

Very truly yours,

John W. Clark
Commissioner of Pensions
By Margaret W. Arnold, Clerk

Transfer of Pensions from Jefferson County, to Clinch County.

Georgia, Jefferson County

I, the undersigned, do certify that Mrs. Adeline Farmer now a Widow Pensioner of this county, is on the Regular Pension Roll and drew a pension of Fifty & 00/100 Dollars for the 1st Quarter 1929. The pension was granted in 1920, on the service of her husband L. D. Farmer, deceased, of Company B; 27th Battalion Georgia Infantry, Confederate States Army, who enlisted July 25, 1864, date of Discharge not given, the said L. D. Farmer was married to Miss Adeline Atwell Mch 1875.

Proven by R. E. Farmer witness and the record.

Given under my hand and official seal, this the 1st day of May 1929.

Ordinary, L. S.

State of Georgia
Pension Department
Atlanta

May 3, 1929

Hon. Louisa Wright
Ordinary of Jefferson County
Louisville, Ga.

Dear dear Judge:

Your letter of May 1, has been received and the name of Mrs. Adeline Farmer has been transferred to the Clinch County roll as requested.

Referring to the Company and Regiment of the two soldiers mentioned, B. P. Padgett was placed on the pension roll in 1922 as a member of Co. F, 19th S. C.

D. J. Thompson was placed on the pension roll in 1910 as a member of Co. B, 27th Ga. Battalion, Ga. Inf. C. S. A.

With kind regards,

Very truly yours,

John W. Clark
Commissioner of Pensions
By Margaret W. Arnold, Clerk

May 13, 1933

Judge Louisa M. Wright, Ordinary
Jefferson County, Georgia
Louisville, Georgia

In Re: Transfer of Mrs. Mary C. Grubbs, Pensioner from Columbia County

Dear Judge Wright:

I have your letter of May 9th, relative to a transfer of Mrs. Mary C. Grubbs, Pensioner, to Jefferson County.

I am enclosing the transfer requested in your letter and by Mrs. Mary C. Grubbs in a letter of May 9th.

With kind regards,

I am, yours respectfully,

G. S. Phillips, Ordinary

Transfer of Pensions from Columbia to Jefferson County.

Georgia, Columbia County

I, the undersigned, do certify that Mrs. Mary C. Grubbs now a Widow Pensioner of this County, is on the Columbia County Pension Roll and drew a pension of Three hundred Sixty Dollars for 1932. The pension was granted in 1922, on the service, or disability, of R. H. Grubbs of Co. G, 5th Ga. Regiment, who enlisted on the __ day of ___ 1861, and was discharged on the __ day of ___ 186_. He was married to Mary E. Anderson on December 13, 1874.

Proven by Record in Ordinary's Office, Columbia Co., Witnesses.

Given under my hand and official seal, this the 13th day of May, 1933.

G. S. Phillips, (L. S.), Ordinary

NOTE: The Ordinary making the transfer should forward this transfer by mail direct to the Ordinary of the County to which the transfer is made, and each Ordinary should report the transfer on the "Deceased, Removed, and Transferred" Blank.

Filed in office May 15th, 1933. Louisa M. Wright, Ordinary

119

April 21, 1934

Mrs. Jane Irby
Avera, Georgia

Dear Mrs. Irby:

As requested by you, I am today forwarding to Hon. Louisa M. Wright the necessary form to have your name transferred to the Jefferson County roll, and requesting that you be paid your March Pension in Louisville.

Please get in touch with Miss Wright relative to future pension payments.

Yours very truly,

Oswell R. Eve
Ordinary, Richmond County

CC: Hon. Louisa M. Wright, Ordinary

Transfer of Pensions from Richmond to Jefferson County.

Georgia, Richmond County

I, the undersigned, do certify that Jane Irby now a widow Pensioner of this County, is on the widow's Pension Roll and drew a pension of Sixty Dollars for January & February 1934. The pension was granted in 1927, on the service, or disability, of A. J. Irby of Co. I, 28th Ga. Regiment, who enlisted on the __ day of ___ 1861, and was discharged on the __ day of ___ 186_. He was married to Mary E. Anderson on December 13, 1874.

Proven by Record in Ordinary's Office, Columbia Co., Witnesses.

Given under my hand and official seal, this the 20th day of April 1934.

Oswell R. Eve (L. S.), Ordinary

NOTE: The Ordinary making the transfer should forward this transfer by mail direct to the Ordinary of the County to which the transfer is made, and each Ordinary should report the transfer on the "Deceased, Removed, and Transferred" Blank.

Pension Roll 1890-1914

The original record is a pre-printed ledger microfilmed by the Genealogical Society of Salt Lake City in 1958 in the offices of the Court of Ordinary in Louisville. The notation on the box holding the microfilm reel at the Georgia Archives indicates the roll is dated 1890-1952; however, the original record only covers the period from 1890 to 1914. On the inside cover of the ledger, the clerk wrote

> *1907*
> *58 Indigent Sol.*
> *14 Soldiers*
> *18 Indigent widows*
> *12 widows*
> *102*

The ledger contains five separate lists: disabled or invalid soldiers, indigent soldiers, indigent soldiers in 1910, widows of deceased soldiers, and indigent widows, each list detailing the annual payments made to the pensioners from 1890 through 1914. The Notes column indicates the annual pension amount and the first and last year payments were made. Often the clerk noted the death of the pensioner, sometimes recording the actual date of death. During this period, the Ordinary made one annual payment to each pensioner early in the year, usually in January. When a pensioner moved into or out of the county, the clerk noted the county from or to which the pensioner transferred. The clerk also sometimes noted the birth year of the pensioner.

Disabled or Invalid Soldiers Rolls

Name	Co.	Regiment	Disability	Witnesses	Notes
Adams, W. B.	E	48 Ga	arm disabled	J. W. Cheatham, L. B. McDaniel, W. Screven	Paid $25 1891-92. Dead.
Adams, W. B.			disabled hand $25		
Bell, Green J.	G	57 Ga	leg	S. T. Joseay, John C. King, L. G. Greenway, J. D.	Paid $50 1891-1899. Transferred to Washington County.

121

Name	Co.	Regiment	Disability	Witnesses	Notes
				Wright, MD	
Brown, W. A.	G	38 Ga	arm disabled	J. R. Powell, MD, T. F. Caulk, S. A. Leonard	Paid $50 1890-1899.
Becton, Curran	B	1 Ga	disabled leg	John Durst, C. F. Miller, W. C. Poland	Paid $50 1895-1902, Home.
Brown, Pat M.	C	20 Ga	arm disabled	W. C. Poland, T. F. Caulk, Ord.	Paid $50 1891-1899. Dead.
Beall, S. S.	C	20 Ga	arm disabled	W. C. Poland, W. G. Walden, G. W. McHatty	Paid $50 1899-1908.
Carr, Thos. A.	I	3 Ga	loss of leg	T. F. Caulk, A. R. Aldred	Transferred from Emanuel County. Paid $100 1904-1914.
Cain, J. G.	I	28 Ga	leg	W. R. Harvey, Geo. L. Cain	Paid $50 1897-1898. Grand Jury '98, Reinstated 1900.
Dawson, Jas. B.	F	Cobb's Legion, Hampton's Brigade	disabled arm	T. F. Caulk	Paid $50 1904. Dead.
Fields, W. J.	E	48 Ga	shot in knee	W. W. Rhodes	Paid $50 1901-1913. Transferred to Sold. Transferred to Bartow County.
Gainer, E. J.	F	8 Ga	body	Alex Avera,	Paid $590 1890-1903.

Name	Co.	Regiment	Disability	Witnesses	Notes
			wound	L. Kitchens	Dead
Glover, J. T.	B	22 Ga	body wound	Thos. Neal, S. R. Rayburn	Paid $50 1897-1913. Transferred to Soldiers of 1910. Born 1837.
Grant, E. J.			body wound		Paid $50 1905-1907.
Hooks, B. A.	B	59 Ga	Dead		Paid $100 1890-1992.
Howard, Jeremiah	G	38 Ga	arm disabled	J. W. Brinson	Paid 450 1890-1897. Transferred to Bulloch County. Paid $50 1900-1901. Transferred to Richmond County.
Hudson, H. J.	G	38 Ga	leg	J. W. Brinson, J. G. Worrill	Paid 450 1890-1897. Transferred to Johnson County.
Hinton, J. M.	F	10 Ga	shoulder and arm wound	W. E. Spier, H. A. Thomas	Paid $50 1902-1914. Born 1837.
Hooks, B. A.			lost leg $100		
King, J. H.	D	15 Ga	disabled leg	T. F. Caulk	Transferred from Hancock County. Paid $50 1896. Transferred to Hancock County.
Lively, Jno. G.	H	48 Ga	lost 3 fingers	T. F. Caulk	Paid $15 1894-1899. Transferred to Burke County.
McNeeley, T. M.	E	48 Ga	wound in head	L. B. McDaniel, G. T. Brown, MD, E. J. Attaway, MD	Paid $50 1905-1908. Born 1841.

Name	Co.	Regiment	Disability	Witnesses	Notes
McDaniel, L. B.	E	48 Ga	disabled arm	E. J. Attaway, MD, G. T. Brown, MD, F. M. McNeeley	Paid $50 1905-1912. Dead 1912. Born 1838.
McGahee, Jno. M.	F	8 Ga	leg	E. J. Gaines, W. T. Harrison, A. A. Stencil	Paid $50 1900-1908. Dead. Born 1838.
Palmer, E.	E	Cobb's Legion	body Wound	Theodore Daniel	Paid $50 1890-1913. Transferred to Soldiers of 1910. Born 1838.
Phillips, W. H.	A	48 Ga	leg	A. H. Walton	Transferred from Richmond County. Paid $50 1897-1906. Dead. Born 1845.
Phillips, Wm	A	48 Ga	body wound	W. F. Fagle, J. L. Fagle	Paid $50 1898-1904. Dead.
Pope, B. B.	I	28 ga	lost one finger	W. H. Douglas	Paid $5 1890-1894.
Pool, W. P. S.	I	1 Ga	body wound	Geo. M. Hood	Paid $50 1890-1893.
Pope, B. B.	I	28 Ga	lost finger $5		
Pool, W. P. S.	I	1 Ga	body wound $50		
Quincy, G. W.	B	27 Ga	disease	W. J. Rhodes, MD, S. M. Clark	Paid $50 1903-1912. Transferred to Soldiers of 1912. Born 1840.
Rayburn, S. R.	A	48 Ga	hand and bowels	E. G. Scruggs	Paid $25 1890-1900. Increased. Paid $50 1901-1913. Died Dec.

Name	Co.	Regiment	Disability	Witnesses	Notes
					1912. Reported on Roll 1913. Born 1836.
Sanders, Wm	D	2 Ga	leg and lost finger	T. F. Caulk, J. W. Meeks	Transferred from Richmond County. Paid $50 1897-1902. Transferred to, Richmond County.
Swan, T. E.	G	38 Ga	useless arm	J. B. Stewart, L. C. Stewart	Dead.
Thomas, J. L.	L	Cobb's Legion	arm disabled	L. D. Johnson	Paid $50 1890-1903. Dead.
Vause, W. A.	I	28 Ga	lost leg $100	T. F. Caulk	Paid $100 1890-1914. Born 1838.
Walden, W. G.	C	20 Ga	body wound	S. S. Beall, W. C. Poland, G. W. McCatty	Paid $50 1898-1905.
Wiggins, E. M.	B	59 Ga	arm	Stephen May, B. F. Bridges, J. T. Arnason	Paid $50 1890-1905.
Wood, J. A.	B	22 Ga	body wound	T. W. Neal, J. T. Glover, L. Kitchens	Paid $50 1900-1913. Died July 1913. Born 1838.
Young, C. W.	H	63 Ga	disabled foot. Struck by minie ball while washing peas, preparing dinner	N. Ellis, J. H. Polhill, R. A. Diche	Paid $25 1892-1908. Transferred. Born 1825.

Indigent Soldiers Pension Roll

Name	Co.	Regiment	Enlist.	Cause	Witnesses	Notes
Arrington, S. A.	B	59 Ga	1862	infirmity, poverty, & age	J. J. Cato, L. C. Warren	Discharged at Appomattox. Paid $60 1902-1914. Born 1838.
Atkinson, E. H.	I	2 Ga	1864	infirmity & poverty	E. H. Bowelling, C. H. Raley, MD	Discharged at Atlanta. Paid $60 1906-1907. Born 1848.
Allen, G. R.	E	1 Ga	1861	age & poverty	A. Youngblood, P. R. Tolliver	Discharged at Augusta. Paid $60 1906-1913. Dead Oct. 1913. Born 1840.
Agerton, E. A.						Paid $60 1911. Transferred from Richmond book.
Barksdale, P. H.						Transferred from McDuffie County '05. Paid $60 1906.
Brown, W. Y.	E	48 Ga	1862	blindness & poverty	C. R. Josey, MD, A. G. Powell	Discharged at Appomattox. Paid $60 1905-1913 and Paid $100 1914. Born 1847.
Beasley, S. F.	F	8 Ga	1862	age & poverty	J. C. Raley, MD, S. T. Hadden	On detail at end of war. Paid $60 1905-1914. Born 1835.
Beasley, Abram	G	1 Ga		infirmity & age		Served 2 years. Paid $60 1904-1907. Dead 9 Jan 1908. Born 1825.

Name	Co.	Regiment	Enlist.	Cause	Witnesses	Notes
Bedgood, J.	F	45 Ga	1862	infirmity, age & poverty		Paid $60 1902-1914. Born 1834.
Barrow, Henry	G	2 Ga	1862	infirmity, poverty & age	Willis Arrington, J. D. Wallace	Discharged April 1865 at Honey Hill, South Carolina. Dead.
Beddingfield, H. J.	E	48 Ga	1862	age & poverty	J. W. Jones, G. F. Brown	Furloughed 1865. Paid $60 1902-1911. Dead 4 Jun 1911. Born 1838.
Beasley, B.	G	38 Ga	1861	infirmity & poverty	H. Howard, J. W. Pilcher	Discharged 1865 at Surrender. Paid $60 1906-1907.
Baslick, J. R.	B	14 Ga	11 Jul 1861	infirmity & poverty	R. G. Cheatham, B. J. Aycock	Discharged 26 Apr 1865. Paid $60 1907-1914.
Beall, W. H.	I	28 Ga		infirmity & poverty	John L. Williams	Discharged Greensboro, North Carolina. Paid $60 1908-1914.
Covington, V. C.	I	28 Ga	Aug 1861	infirmity & poverty	J. L. Williams, J. C. Raley, MD	Surrendered Apr 1865 Bushill, North Carolina. Paid $60 1896-1898 and 1901-1912. Died 22 May 1912. Born 1835.
Carroll, John	F	10 Ga	Jun 1861	age & poverty	J. D. Boney, Pierce Hubert, MD	1865 at Fort Delaware. Paid $60 1897-1902. Dead.
Cowart, S. L.	L	Cobb's	1862	infirmity, poverty, &	W. W. Fleming, W.	Surrendered Apr 1865. Paid $60

Name	Co.	Regiment	Enlist.	Cause	Witnesses	Notes
		Legion		age	J. Rhodes, MD	1902-1905.
Covington, W.	H	63 Ga	Aug 1862	age & poverty	T. E. Walden, W. J. Rhodes, MD	Detail service Hospital 9 Apr 1865. Paid $60 1900.
Camp, Zebedie	H	2 Ga	10 Feb 1863	indigent	G. A. Wheeler	Surrendered 21 Apr 1865. Paid $60 1908-1914. Transferred from Warren County 17 Dec 1907.
Clay, L. B.	C	13 Tenn	1862	infirmity & poverty	W. C. Clay	Paid $60 1909-1914. McEwen County, Texas.
Cowart, F. L.	C	2 Ga	1863	infirmity & poverty	G. W. Beddingfield	Surrendered Apr 1865. Paid $60 1909-1912.
Dye, M. G.						Dead.
Dixon, W. R.	C	32 Ga	12 May 1862	infirmity & poverty	H. Wemberly, C. H. Raley	Surrendered Apr 1865 Greensboro, North Carolina. Transferred from Glascock County. Paid $60 1903, Dead.
Dixon, Nehemiah	I	28 Ga	22 May 1864	infirmity & poverty	J. L. Neal, G. W. Kelley, MD	Surrendered 1865. Paid $60 1896-1914. Born 1838.
Dunaway, G. W.	H	50 Ga	Apr 1862	infirmity & poverty	J. W. Pilcher, MD, C. H. Raley	Discharged Dec 1864 Savannah. Dead.
Dye, B. G.	Burks	2 Ga		infirmity & poverty	J. W. Pilcher, MD, C. H. Raley	Surrendered 1865 Appomattox. Paid $60 1899-

Name	Co.	Regiment	Enlist.	Cause	Witnesses	Notes
						1901.
Diehl, R. A.	D	Atty Lt. Guards	1863	infirmity & poverty	M. H. Hopkins, J. A. Wright	Appomattox
Daniels, Thos.		48 Ga		age & poverty	Glascock County	Paid $60 1905-1911. Dead 20 Jan 1911. Born [smudge]
Dye, John E.	D	2 Ga	Jul-64	infirmity & poverty	J. R. Rollins, Burke County	Paid $60 1910-1914.
Easler, John						Paid $60 1902. Transferred to McDuffie County.
Ferrell, Thos.	A	48 Ga	Mar 1862	infirmity, poverty & age	S. R. Rayburn, W. J. Rhodes	Paid $60 1902-1906. Born 1840.
Fleming, S. P.	F	Cobb's Legion	May 1862	infirmity & age	W. W. Fleming, W. J. Rhodes, MD	Paid $60 1903-1911. Dead Jul 1910. Born 1835.
Goodwin, J. D.	D	12 Ga	1861	infirmity & poverty	J. L. Pickles, W. Arrington	10 Jul 1864 was held as prisoner, 20 May 1865 Paroled. Paid $60 1907-1914.
Gordon, Samuel J.	F	Cobb's Legion	Mar 1862	infirmity & poverty	W. C. Houser, J. M. Kennedy	Served until 1865. Paid 1907-1910. Dead 7 Jul 1910.
Gordon, James	F	Cobb's Legion		infirmity, poverty, age & partly blind	W. B. Johnson, J. D. Knight, MD	Surrendered at Greensboro, North Carolina. Dead.
Goodowns, John	G	2 Ga	23 May 1864	infirmity, poverty &	J. C. Raley, T. S. Roney	Discharged Augusta, 1865.

Name	Co.	Regiment	Enlist.	Cause	Witnesses	Notes
				age		Paid $60 1896.
Harverly, Whit	K	14 SC	1861	infirmity & poverty	G. T. Brown, MD, N. T. McDaniel	Discharged 1865, Appomattox. Paid $60 1905-1910. Dead 10 May 1911. Came to Georgia 1892. Born 1845.
Harden, C. W.	F	62 Ga	1862	infirmity & poverty	C. J. Fields, C. W. Gilcheris, MD	In prison at Point Lookout, discharged at Augusta. Paid $60 1900-1905. Born 1847.
Howard, Thos.	E	27 Ga	2 May 1864	infirmity & poverty	W. H. Lucky, C. H. Raley, MD	Discharged 1865, Aiken, South Carolina. Paid $60 1896-1905. Born 1847.
Hatcher, Robt.	B	19 SC	1862	infirmity, poverty & age	T. W. Getzen, W. J. Rhodes, MD	Discharged at close of war. Paid $60 1903. Dead Aug 1907. Later 1903.
Hudson, J. C.	G	38 Ga	1861	infirmity & poverty	Willis Arrington, A. S. Smith	Discharged account of Rheumatism 1862. Paid $60 1907.
Hall, Benj.	F	8 Ga Cav	Nov 1861	infirmity & poverty	N. T. Harmon	Discharged 19 May 1865. Paid $60 1907-1911. Dead 3 Apr 1911.
Ivey, G. H. L.	A	7 Ga	1863	infirmity & poverty	J. C. Reagin, W. J. Rhodes	Furloughed Nov 1864 Greensboro, North Carolina. Paid $60 1903-

Name	Co.	Regiment	Enlist.	Cause	Witnesses	Notes
						1914. Born 1826.
Irby, W. R.	I	28 Ga	1 Aug 1861	infirmity & poverty	V. C. Covington, C. W. Kitchens	Discharged 1865 Augusta. Glascock County.
Irby, S. R.	G	2 Ga	1864	infirmity, poverty & age	J. C. Raley, MD, T. S. Roney	Discharged 1865. Paid $60 1896.
Ivey, B. H.	H	22 Ga	Aug 1861			Originally from Wilkes County. Discharged 9 Apr 1865 Appomattox. Paid $60 1908-1914. Transferred from Dodge County 23 Dec 1907.
Jones, Jake A.	D	City Guard	Jan 1863	infirmity, blindness & age	A. A. Charne, MD, W. B. Holmes	Discharged Macon, Georgia 1865. Paid $60 1898. Transferred to Emmanuel County.
James, J. A.	C	20 Ga		infirmity & poverty		Served 3 years, 8 months. Paid $60 1899-1914. Born 1832.
Johnson, J. M.	F	Cables	May 1862	infirmity & poverty	J. D. Wight, MD, G. W. Kelley	Discharged Hillsboro, North Carolina 1865.
James, L. C.		Wheeler's Dragoons	Nov 1862	infirmity & poverty	John Harris	Surrendered Greensboro, North Carolina. Paid $60 1908-1911. Died 20 Nov 1910. Paid

Name	Co.	Regiment	Enlist.	Cause	Witnesses	Notes
						widow.
Kendrick, G. W.	E	48 Ga	Mar 1862	infirmity & poverty	J. W. Cheatham, J. W. Pilcher, MD	Discharged Apr 1865 Appomattox. Paid $60 1902-1910. Died 7 Jul 1910. Born 1831.
Kendrick, B. J.	F	12 Ga	1 Mar 1862	infirmity & poverty	J. W. Pilcher, J. W. Raley, MD	Surrendered Greensboro, North Carolina. Paid 1896-1898. Transferred to Burke County.
King, T. G.	B	55 Ga	1861	infirmity & poverty		Transferred from Hancock County. Paid $60 1898-1907. Transferred to Emmanuel County 31 Jan 1908. Born 1843.
Kitchens, Laurence	B	22 Ga	18 Jul 1861	blindness & poverty	M. E. Irby, H. Raley, MD	Discharged Apr 1865 Appomattox. Paid $60 1901-1914. Born 1840.
Kendrick, J. P.	C	20 Ga	1862	infirmity & poverty	J. W. Weeks	At home at close of war. Paid $60 1905-1914. Born [smudge]
Kennedy, Jim	F	Cobb's Legion	Mar 1862	infirmity & poverty	S. J. Jordon	Discharged Apr 1865. Paid $60 1910-1914.
Le Fever, John	E	28 Ga	Aug 1861	infirmity & poverty	W. T. Roney, MD, J. C. Raley	In prison Apr 1865. Paid $60 1896-1914. Born 1840.

Name	Co.	Regiment	Enlist.	Cause	Witnesses	Notes
Landrum, P. H.	A	27 Ga	1863	infirmity & poverty	J. F. Brawell, W. T. Roney, MD	Discharged Apr 1865 Greensboro, North Carolina. Paid $60 1903-1904.
Lowe, J. E.	A	63 Ga & 38 Ga		infirmity & poverty	G. W. Kelley, J. D. Night	Served 4 years until surrender. Paid $60 1896-1897.
Moxley, A. S.	B	22 Ga	Jun 1862	infirmity & poverty	S. D. Gordon, Samuel J. Gordon	Discharged Apr 1865. Paid $60 1907-1911. Dead. Paid funeral expenses.
McVey, W. C.	E	32 Ga	1863	infirmity, poverty & age	from Montgomery 1906.	Paid $60 1907. Transferred to Washington County 21 Dec 1907. Born 1827.
Mead, W. E.		Howell's Battery	1864	infirmity & poverty	W. J. Rhodes, MD, Wm Oxford	Discharged Apr 1865 Macon. Paid $60 1905-1914.
McGinnis, D. B.	C	45 Ga	1862	age & poverty	E. H. Owens, J. D. Knight	Discharged 1865, and served 2 years, 4 months. Paid $60 1896-1904. Dead. Born 1844.
Mulling, E. James		Howell's Battery		infirmity & poverty		Surrendered at Macon, Georgia. Paid $60 1899-1914. Born 1842.
Murphy, J. H.	C	20 Ga	Apr 1861	blindness & poverty	H. M. Perdue, C. H. Raley, MD	Discharged in Virginia 1865. Paid $60 1896-1914. Born 1829.

Name	Co.	Regiment	Enlist.	Cause	Witnesses	Notes
McNair, S. J.	E	48 Ga	1862	age & poverty	L. B. McDaniel, W. J. Rodes, MD	Surrendered at Appomattox. Paid $60 1902-1904. Dead
Marsh, John	A	48 Ga	May 1862	infirmity, poverty & age	G. W. Rea, W. T. Roney, MD	Served until surrender. Paid $60 1902-1914. Born 1839.
McNeely, Denny	A	Clark	1863	age & poverty		Discharged at Atlanta Apr 1865. Paid $60 1896-1898 and 1903-1906. Dead. Born 1817.
Mathews, M. F.	I	28 Ga	May 1864	infirmity & poverty	H. Mathews, J. W. Pilcher	Discharged at Augusta. Paid $60 1896-1898 and 1903-1914. Born 1846.
Newman, E. F.	E	28 Ga	Aug 1861	infirmity & poverty	Thos. Dismuke, W. T. Roney	Discharged Apr 1865 Greensboro, North Carolina. Paid $60 1902. Transferred to Richmond County. Paid $60 1905-1914. Born 1840.
Owens, E. H.	C	45 Al	Mar 1865	infirmity & poverty	D. B. McGinnis, C. W. Kitchens	Discharged Greensboro, North Carolina 1865. Dead
Oxford, William		Howell's Battery	1861	infirmity & poverty	W. J. Bell, J. W. Kitchens	Discharged at Macon 1865. Paid $60 1906-1914. Transferred to Emmanuel County. Born

Name	Co.	Regiment	Enlist.	Cause	Witnesses	Notes
						1843.
Phillips, James	G	1 Ga	1864	infirmity & poverty	J. F. Rivers, R. T. Barton, MD	Discharged Apr 1865 Augusta. Paid $60 1904-1907. Born 1840.
Peebles, J. L.	Light Atty	Apr 1862			W. C. Langham, W. T. Roney, MD	Discharged 9 Apr 1865 Appomattox. Paid $60 1901-1907. Transferred to Glascock County 16 Jan 1908. Born 1840.
Pope, B. B.	F	32 Ga	1862	infirmity & poverty	J. C. Raley, MD, T. S. Roney, MD	Served until 1865 surrender. Paid $60 1896-1905 and 1909-1911. Dead 11 Feb 1911. Born 1837.
Pope, R. F.	G	2 Ga	1864	infirmity, poverty & age	J. C. Raley, MD, T. S. Roney, MD	Served until 1865, surrendered at Augusta. Paid $60 1896-1901. Transferred to Irwin County.
Parish, Middleton		Brown's Cables		age & poverty	J. W. Pilcher, MD, C. H. Raley	Discharged 1865 Augusta. Paid $60 1899. Dead.
Prescott, J. P.						Paid $60 1899. Dead.
Prescott, J. T.	G	28 Ga		age & poverty	John Russell, J. W. Pilcher, MD	Served until 1865 surrender. Paid $60 1898.
Page, Joseph Y.	E	48 Ga	Mar	blindness	A. A. Charne, W.	Discharged 9 Apr 1865

Name	Co.	Regiment	Enlist.	Cause	Witnesses	Notes
			1862	& poverty	B. Holmes	Appomattox. Paid $60 1901-1903. Dead.
Page, W. H.	B	20 Ga	1861	age & poverty	Z. D. Bowen, G. T. Browen	Discharged at Petersburg 1864. Paid $60 1903-1914. Born 1835.
Paradise, W. D.	G	57 Ga	1862	age & poverty	B. G. Greenway, C. R. Jorey	In prison at Point Lookout at close of war. Paid $60 1903-1904. Dead.
Peebles, Thomas	I	63 Ga	1863	age & poverty	J. W. Pilcher, MD, C. W. Young	In 1865 on detail service. Paid $60 1905-1914. Born 1830.
Reese, M. E.	B	48 Ga	Mar 1862	infirmity & poverty	T. J. Dickson, W. T. Roney, MD	Served until 1865 surrender. Paid $60 1900-1909. Dead 10 Sep 1909. Born 1826.
Russell, John	G	2 Ga	May 1864	infirmity & poverty	W. R. Hampton, W. V. Walden	On furlough in 1865. Paid $60 1897-1901. Dead.
Roberson, W.	I	28 Ga	Jul 1862	age & poverty	J. W. Pilcher, MD, C. H. Raley	Discharged sick 1863. Paid $60 1899-1900. Transferred to Warren County.
Rosier, Stephen	C	20 Ga	14 Jun 1861	age & poverty	A. G. Carswell, MD, G. W. Kelley	Served until 1865 surrender. Paid $60 1896-1897.
Rhodes, Richard	B	22 Ga	Apr 1862	blindness & poverty	L. Kitchens, W. T. Roney	In prison in 1865. Paid $60 1903-

Name	Co.	Regiment	Enlist.	Cause	Witnesses	Notes
						1905. Born 1837.
Roberts, J. W.	B	27 Ga	Sep 1863	infirmity & poverty	W. J. Rhodes, MD, G. W. Quincy	Discharged 1865 Augusta. Paid $60 1906-1908. Born 1845.
Rooks, M.	C	27 Ga	1863	infirmity & poverty	J. W. Pilcher, MD, G. R. Cook	Home on furlough 1865. Paid $60 1906-1908. Transferred to Richmond County. Born 1846.
Rogers, S. B.						Transferred from Wilkes County. Paid $60 1909-1912. Transferred to Glascock County 20 Dec 1912.
Reynolds, Geo.						Paid $60 1911-1914.
Stewart, L. C.	G	38 Ga	1862	infirmity & poverty	J. W. Meeks, J. W. Pilcher, MD	1865 at home paroled. Paid $60 1905-1914.
Screws, Jas. A.	F	62 Ga	1862	age, infirmity & poverty	N. T. Hannah, W. B. Holmes, MD	Discharged 1865 Belfield, North Carolina. Paid $60 1905-1911. Dead. Paid funeral. 15 Jun 1911. Born 1840.
Saxon, R. Y.	A	3 Ga	Apr 1861	infirmity & poverty	T. W. Burton, W. J. Rhodes	Discharged 1865 Farmville, Virginia. Paid $60 1902. Transferred to Burke County.

Name	Co.	Regiment	Enlist.	Cause	Witnesses	Notes
Sammons, H. L.	B	22 Ga	1861	infirmity & poverty	J. W. Pilcher, MD, C. H. Raley	Served until 1865 surrender. Paid $60 1896-1914. Born 1838.
Scarboro, Wm	H	48 Ga	1862	age & poverty	Virgil Powell, C. R. Josey	On furlough at surrender 1865. Paid $60 1897-1910. Dead. Mar 1911. Born 1837.
Screws, J. A.	E	48 Ga	9 Mar 1862	infirmity, poverty & blindness	J. W. Cheatham, A. A. Chance	Served until surrender. Paid $60 1897-1912. Dead. 16 Aug 1912. Born 1832.
Stewart, A. A.	F	8 Ga	Aug 1861	infirmity, poverty & age	J. C. Little, C. H. Raley, MD	Served until close of war. Paid $60 1900-1914. Age 75 in 1906.
Swift, T. G.	I	Ga State Line	1 Jan 1863	blindness & poverty	E. L. Gaines, W. T. Roney, MD	Discharged May 1863 sick. Paid $60 1900-1906. Born 1831.
Stevens, W. L.		Howell's		infirmity & poverty	J. H. Coleman, W. J. Rhodes	Surrendered Macon 1865. Paid $60 1900-1901. Asylum.
Stewart, J. B.	G	38 Ga	1862	infirmity & poverty	Willis Arrington, C. H. Raley, MD	Discharged Spotsylvania Court House, Virginia. Paid $60 1900-1911. dead. Paid funeral expenses. Born 1834.
Smith, Wm	F	62 Ga	1862	infirmity & poverty	J. C. Little, J. W. Pilcher, MD	Discharged near Petersburg, Virginia. Paid $60 1903-1914.

Name	Co.	Regiment	Enlist.	Cause	Witnesses	Notes
						Born 1842.
Stewart, Wm	G	38 Ga	1861	infirmity & poverty	J. B. Stewart	In prison at Elmira, New York. Paid $60 1906. Dead. Born 1838.
Thomas, John B.		Howell's Battery	1862	age, infirmity & poverty	W. J. Bell	Discharged Apr 1865. Paid $60 1908-1910. Dead Aug 1911.
Tucker, J. W.	A	63 Ga		blindness & poverty	E. J. Attaway, A. G. Carswell	Served 3 years until surrender.
Upton, J. F.	I	11 Ga	1861	infirmity & poverty	A. R. Aldred	Discharged Apr 1865. Paid 460 1910-1914.
Underwood, Geo.	F	8 Ga	Jun 1862	blindness & poverty	C. W. Kitchens, G. W. Kelley	Discharged Augusta. Paid $60 1896-1907. Born 1834.
Williford, H. P.	B	22 Ga		blindness & poverty		Served 4 years. Paid $60 1904-1906. Dead. Cant his funeral in 1907. Born 1833.
Whitehead, Robt.	G	38 Ga	1861	infirmity, poverty & age	J. W. Pilcher, C. H. Raley	Discharged at Richmond, Virginia. Paid $60 1896-1901. Dead. Born 1827.
Williams, J. L.	I	28 Ga	1862	infirmity, poverty & age	J. C. Raley, MD, T. S. Roney	Discharged at Augusta Apr 1865. Paid $60 1896-1912. Dead Aug 1912.

Name	Co.	Regiment	Enlist.	Cause	Witnesses	Notes
Watkins, J. B.	D	28 Ga	Mary 1864	age & poverty	Pierce Hubert, MD, J. D. Night, MD	Surrendered 9 Apr 1865. Paid $60 1899. Dead.
Wilkinson, Jesse	I	28 Ga	1861	infirmity, poverty & age	J. W. Pilcher, MD, C. H. Raley	Served until 1865. Paid $60 1896-1901. Transferred to Johnson County.
Williams, R. E.	I	28 Ga	Aug 1861	infirmity & poverty	V. C. Corrington, J. C. Raley	Discharged 1865 Bush Hill, North Carolina. Paid $30 1897. Paid $60 1898-1914. Born 1839.
Weeks, J. W.	G	38 Ga	1861	infirmity & poverty		Transferred from Burke County. Paid $60 1900-1912. Born 1839.
Wimberly, Homer	E & C	32 Ga	May 1862	infirmity, poverty & age	J. D. Night, MD, W. J. Rhoder	Discharged Apr 1865 Augusta. Paid $60 1902-1914. Born 1833.
Williams, J. F.	I	28 Ga	Mar 1862	infirmity & poverty	B. B. Pope, J. C. Raley, MD	March 1865 in prison. Paid $60 1902-1904. Dead.
Williams, S. A.	I	28 Ga		infirmity & poverty	B. B. Pope, J. C. Raley, MD	Discharged Apr 1865 Greensboro, North Carolina. Paid $60 1902-1914. Born 1838.
Way, Wm F.	G	38 Ga	1861	blindness & poverty	A. S. Smith, W. J. Rhoder, MD, L. A. Williams, J. C. Raley,	Discharged Richmond, Virginia. Paid $60 1903-1907. Dead Aug 1907.

Name	Co.	Regiment	Enlist.	Cause	Witnesses	Notes
					MD	Born 1833.
Williams, Jno. L.	I	28 Ga	1861	infirmity & poverty		Discharged Apr 1865 Greensboro, North Carolina. Paid $60 1905-1914. Born 1841.
Wurts, B. E.	E	Marine Corps	Nov 1864	infirmity & poverty	W. H. Harris	Discharged Apr 1865 Greensboro, North Carolina. Paid $60 1907-1914. Dead 14 Jan 1914.
Young, Thomas M.	Dead	Gun Boat	1862	infirmity, poverty & age	J. W. Pilcher, MD, C. H. Raley	In prison at close of war. Dead.

Indigent Soldiers Pension Roll 1910

Name	Co.	Regiment	Enl.	Cause	Witnesses	Notes
Aldred, W. M.						Paid $60 1911-1914.
Allen, D. G. D.	A	Rowland's Battery	Feb 1863		J. M. Stapleton, J. R. Harris, Willis Arrington	Surrendered Macon Apr 1865. Paid $60 1911-1914
Anderson, Jno.	G	12 Ga	Jul 1864		J. J. Phillips, A. P. Rivers	Surrendered Augusta 8 Apr 1865. Paid $60 1911-1914.
Culver, B. C.						Paid $60 1911. Dead 2 Oct 1911.
Beasley, Thos. G.	E	27 Ga	Oct 1864		A. J. Mathews, J. L. Watson, Emmanuel County	Mar 1865 was sent off from his command salt works, reached it & at Greensboro, North Carolina surrendered with it. Paid $60 1912-1914
Arrington, Willis						Paid $60 1913-1914.
Farmer, J. V.						Paid $60 1911-1914.
Fountain, J. A.						Paid $60 1911-1914.
Folks, W. Y.						Paid $60 1914.
Denny, W. A.						Paid $60 1913-1914.
Glover, J. T.						Paid $60 1913-

Name	Co.	Regiment	Enl.	Cause	Witnesses	Notes
						1914.
Guy, Joel						Paid $60 1914.
Gunn, Lewis F.						Paid $60 1911-1914.
Hutto, L. B.						Paid $60 1911-1914.
Hill, M. C., Jr.	B	Howell's Legion				Paid $60 1911-1914.
Ham, Allen P.	E	C. S. Marines				Paid $60 1911-1912. Transferred to Lincoln County 12 Dec 1912.
Harmon, N. T.			.			Paid $60 1911. Dead 28 Oct 1911..
Hall, J. M.						Paid $60 1911-1913. Died July 1913.
Kinmon, J. K.	B	12 Ga Bttn Lt Atty			James Anderson, Bibb County, J. Q. Brassell	Dec 1864 granted sick leave, and was unable to return. Paid $60 1913-1914.
Luckey, W. H.	E	27 Ga	May 1862		James Anderson, Bibb County, J. Q. Brassell	Dec 1864 granted sick leave, and was unable to return. Paid $60 1911-1914.
Murphy, H. D., Rev.	B	12 Ga Bttn Lt Atty	Aug 1863		R. P. Bryan, Washington County, S. M. Clark	Surrendered Savannah Apr 1865. Paid $60 1914.
Perdue, A. M.						Paid $60 1911-

Name	Co.	Regiment	Enl.	Cause	Witnesses	Notes
						1914.
Phillips, S. G.	I	28 Ga				Paid $60 1911-1914.
Morris, W. H.	G	1 SC	Feb 1861		J. B. Hunter, Bamburg, South Carolina, W. L. Phillips, J. A. B. Watkins	Surrendered Appomattox, Virginia Apr 1865. Paid $60 1912-1914.
Roberts, W. L.						Paid $60 1911-1912.
Rains, J. L.	D	27 Ga Bttn	May 1864		L. S. Peel, W. R. Sinquefield, R. A. Ponder	Born 12 Nov 1848 in Washington County. Married Emily Jane McNeely 7 Nov 1892 by Rev. A. J. Jower in Jefferson County. Died 20 Oct 1926 in Jefferson County. About two weeks before surrender granted furlough. Was unable to return. Paid $60 1911-1914.
Quinney, Geo. W.	B	27 Ga	Oct 1863		S. M. Clark, J. H. Polhill, A. L. R. Farmer	Discharged Greensboro, North Carolina, Apr 1865. Paid $60 1911-1914.
Screws, William						Paid $60 1913-1914.

Name	Co.	Regiment	Enl.	Cause	Witnesses	Notes
Smith, S. K.	F	8 Ga Cav	Oct 1864			Surrendered at end of the war. Paid $60 1911. Dead 1911. Paid widow.
Thompson, D. J.		27 Ga Bttn	6 Nov 1864			Surrendered Apr 1865. Paid $60 1911-1914.
T[faint]						Paid $60 1911-1914.
Vause, J. M.	I	28 Ga	10 Sep 1861			Transferred after recovering from wound Co. E, 1st Ga Troops. Dead 15 Dec 1910.
Quinney, Wm J.						Paid $60 1911-1914.

Attached to the pages of the 1910 list are a series of letters and other correspondence.

State of Georgia
Pension Department
Atlanta

December 2, 1929

Hon. Louisa M. Wright
Ordinary of Jefferson County
Louisville, Ga.

My dear Judge:

Your request for the Confederate War record of Allen P. Ham, deceased pensioner of your county, is received, and I take pleasure in furnishing you this record as shown on his application for a pension in 1910.

Allen P. Ham enlisted (was conscripted) June 7, 1863, Camp Randolph (witness says Savannah), Company "E" C. S. Marines, under Commodore Futral. Served with his Command until the surrender at Charlotte, N. C., and he was present.

Assuring you of my pleasure in furnishing you this information, and with kind regards,

Very truly yours,

R. deT. Lawrence
Commissioner of Pensions

Copy to
Mrs. J. S. Harden,
Greensboro, Georgia.

State of Georgia
Pension Department
Atlanta

March 21, 1928

Hon. Louisa M. Wright
Ordinary of Jefferson County
Louisville, Ga.

My dear Judge:

I am in receipt of your inquiry of the 20th instant relative to the war record of Jas. M. Kinman, and it is my pleasure to inform you that his record as shown in his application for a pension states "Company "B", 12th Battalion Georgia Light Infantry."

Very truly yours,

John W. Clark
Commissioner of Pensions

Copy

WAR DEPARTMEN
THE ADJUTANT GENERAL'S OFFICE
WSHINGTON

In reply A. G. 201
Refer to Thompson, David J.   ESA
(5-25-38) ORD

June 1, 1938

Honorable Carl Vinson
House of Representatives

My dear Mr. Vinson:

I have your letter of May 25, 1938, in which you request to be furnished a record of he service of David J. Thompson said to have served in the 27th Georgia Battalion Infantry, Confederate States Army.

The records show that one David __ Thompson, name not found as David J. or D. J. Thompson, private Company B, 27th Battalion Georgia Infantry, Confederate States Army, enlisted November 6, 1864, last roll on file shows him absent sick in hospital. No later record of him has been found.

The collection of Confederate States Army records is incomplete, and the failure to find he complete record of any person thereon is by no means conclusive proof that such person did not serve at some period not covered by the records.

Very respectfully,

E. Alidans
Major General,
The Adjutant General

State of Georgia
Pension Department
Atlanta

July 28, 1931

Hon. Louisa M. Wright
Ordinary of Jefferson County
Louisville, Ga.

Dear Judge:

In response to your request, I submit the following record of a Confederate Soldier:

"James W. Vause, enlisted as a private Co. I, 28th Regt. Ga. Vol. Inf. September 10, 1861. Wounded Fredericksburg, Va. Dec. 13, 1862. Transferred to Co. E, 1st Regt. Troops & Defenses, Macon, Ga., 1864. Absent with Provost Guard, Atlanta, Ga. Dec. 31, 1864." (Washington Record)

With kindest regards,

Your friend,

John J. Hunt
Commissioner of Pensions

Widows of Deceased Soldiers Roll

Widow	Husband	Enl.	Co.	Regiment	Witnesses	Notes
Agerton, Elmira	Wm J. Agerton	Apr 1862	D	48 Ga	Alexander Owen, T. Skinner, J. H. Collis	Killed Gettysburg 2 Jul 1863. Paid $60 1895-1897. Transferred to Burke County.
Beasley, Ellen	Bryant Beasley	May 1864	G	2 Ga	G. M. Beddingfield, W. A. Tarver, J. M. Gordom	Died Macon Hospital Sep 1864. Paid $60 1895-1900. Dead.
Braswell, Judy	Jno. J. Braswell	1862		Howell's Battery	W. J. Bell, Wm Axford, Jno. Thomas	Killed Missionary Ridge 1862. Paid $60 1895-1911. Dead 3 Aug 1911. Married 1854.
Corner, M. A.	J. M. Corner	Apr 1862	C	20	T. J. Wilkerson, N. K. Butler, W. A. Dear	Died 1867 wound and blood poison. Paid $60 1895-1905.
Covington, Susan	V. C. Covington					Paid $60 1914.
Denton, M. A.	Jas. Denton	Mar 1862	A	48 Ga	Hardy Todd, W. W. Moon, J. L. Fagler	Died wounds, Second Manassas. Paid $60 1895-1900. Dead.
Du Priest, Margaret	J. B. Du Priest	Sep 1863	K	50 Ga	A. H. Wooten	Supposed killed Nov 1864. Never returned home. Paid $60 1897-1914. Married 1860.
Davis, Temperance	Thos. L. Davis	Jan 1864	E	Potter Reg.	T. F. Cauk	Died 3 Aug 1864. Transferred from Washington County. Paid $60 1903-1914. Born

Widow	Husband	Enl.	Co.	Regiment	Witnesses	Notes
						1849.
Darby, M. E.	Chas. S. Darby	Jun 1861	A	12 Ga		Died 1864 Gettysburg. Transferred from Sumter County. Paid $60 1899. Transferred to Glynn County.
Deviso, Elizabeth	Jas. M. Deviso	1862	L	Cobb's Legion		Error.
Farron, Catherine	Wm J. Farron	Jan 1862	G	38 Ga	J. W. Brinson, T. E. Swan, Benj. Beasley	Died effects of measles May 1862. Paid $60 1895-1897. Dead.
Hall, M. J.	Wm K. Hall	Mar 1862	E	48 Ga	R. N. Perdue, L. B. McDanel. Wm Scarews	Died 31 Jul 1862 from disease in hospital. Paid $60 1895-1914. Married 1860.
Hadden, Martha	Wm P. Hadden	Aug 1861	I	28 Ga	W. H. Douglas, W. R. Harvey, J. W. P. Whitely	Died R. Hospital Apr 1862. Paid $60 1895-1901. Dead.
Joiner, Ann S.	Malachi Joiner	Apr 1862	E	12 Ga	W. W. Rhodes	Died Frederick City, Maryland 1864. Transferred from Washington County. Paid $60 1901-1902. Transferred to Washington County.
Odom, Sarah A.	Jno. A. Odom	Aug 1861	B	28 Ga	J. C. Tunnille, Henry King,	Died from disease Nov 1861. Dead.

Widow	Husband	Enl.	Co.	Regiment	Witnesses	Notes
					F. N. Arman	
Outten, Caroline	Geo. W. Outten, Sr.	Apr 1862	C	1 Ga	W. D. Dixon, B. A. Grubbs	Died Savannah Sep 1862. Paid $60 1895. Dead.
Perkins, Mary	Robt. D. Perkins	Mar 1862	E	48 Ga	M. W. Rhodes, A. B. Freeman, E. M. Averitt	Died hospital Dec 1862. Paid $60 1901-1905.
Potter, Elizabeth	Edmond Potter	Jul 1864	B	2 Ga	Wm F. Cawley, Benj. Beasley, J. W. Brinson	Died measles Oct 1864. Paid $60 1895. Dead.
Pool, E. A.	Isaac B. Pool	Sep 1861	G	38 Ga	T. E. Swan	Died disease 16 Feb 1862. Dead.
Paradise, Amanda	R. C. Paradise	1862	G	57 Ga	A. H. Mattox	Killed Kennesaw Mountain, Jun 1864. Paid $60 1895-1899. Dead.
Robinson, K. M.	Dempsey Robinson	Aug 1861	I	28 Ga	W. H. Douglas, A. L. Aldred, J. G. Cain, T. D. Smith	Died 22 Feb 1862 from disease. Paid $60 1895-1914. Married 1856.
Rowland, Adaline	Geo. Rowland	Aug 1861	H	14 Ga	Hardy Smith, Ben. Adkins, Elizabeth Hobbs, C. H. Raley	Died from measles Sep 1865. Paid 460 1895-1911. Dead. Married 1857.
Rooks, Julia	Jeremiah Rooks	1861	A	63 Ga		Died at home on sick furlough. Paid $60 1906.
Reid, Mrs. S. J.	Jno. S. Reid	1863		38 Ga		Died 20 Mar 1865 in Smithfield Hospital. Infirmity &

Widow	Husband	Enl.	Co.	Regiment	Witnesses	Notes
						poverty. Paid $60 1912-1914.
Scott, M. E.	Hartwell Scott	Apr 1861	E	15 Ga	H. E. Garrett, Henry Harris, J. J. Fleury	Killed Chickamauga Sept 1863. Paid $60 1895-1909. Married 1855.
Swan, Jane	Henry Swan	Apr 1862	L	Cobb's Legion	S. D. Gordon, L. D. Jackson, J. A. Fleming	Died disease Nov 1864. Paid $60 1895-1906. Dead. Married 1850.
Smith, Sarah	Ethelred A. Smith		H	63 Ga	J. N. Oliphant, N. Ellis, J. W. Brinson	Died from measles Sep 1864. Paid $60 1895-1900. Dead.
Stevens, M. A.	Edward Stevens	Jan 1863	L	Cobb's Legion	Jno. Bargamier, S. L. Cowart, J. B. Watkins	Died from disease Mar 1865. Paid $60 1895-1899. Dead.
Terrell, N. M.	Richard Terrell	May 1864	G	2 Ga	W. R. Thompson, Jno. Russell, Jno. Bargamier	Died from disease July 1864 at Atlanta. Paid $60 1895-1911. Dead 6 Nov 1911. Married 1849.
Thompson, Marga	David J. Thompson	Mar 1862	C	48 Ga	S. E. McNeely, J. H. Cotton, T. N. McNeely	Died R. Hospital Dec 1862. Eresipelas. Paid $60 1895-1900. Dead.
Thompson, E. A.	Solomon Thompson	May 1863	G	2 Ga	J. M. Goodwin, Jno. Russell, J. N. Thompson	Died 1869 wound & disease. Paid $60 1895-1904. Dead.
Vining, Mary	Jasper Vining	May	G	2 Ga	J. M. Goodwin, W.	Died Dec 1864 in hospital at

Widow	Husband	Enl.	Co.	Regiment	Witnesses	Notes
		1863			R. Thompson, Jno. Russell	Augusta from wounds. Paid $60 1895-1907. Married 1861.
Wren, Rebecca	Jeremiah Wren	Aug 1861	I	28 Ga	W. H. Douglas, J. W. P. Whitney, W. R. Harvey	Died Yorktown suddenly 15 Apr 1862. Paid $60 1895-1914. Married 1849.
Whitehead, Susannah	Henry Whitehead	May 1864	E	27 Ga	A. H. Wooten	Died 1869. Paid $60 1898-1914. Married 1863.
Williams, Caroline	J. N. Williams	Jul 1862	F	8 Ga	W. W. Rhodes	Died 1883 of consumption. Paid $60 1897-1898 and 1902-1914. Married 1861.
Wood, Mary E.	Thos. G. Wood	Jun 1862	E	48 Ga	T. M. McNeely, P. Perkins, W. D. Maxley	Died Guard Station, Virginia, disease, Mar 1863. Dead.

Indigent Widows Roll

Widow	Husband	Co.	Regiment	Enl.	Witnesses	Notes
Adams, Eliza	W. B. Adams	E	48 Ga	1862	W. T. Roney, MD, W. W. Terrell, A. R. Alored	Discharged at close of war. Age & poverty. Paid $60 1902-1905.
Darby, Mary	Jerido Darby	H	63 Ga	1862	W. T. Roney, MD, J. C. Roley, Martin G. Dye	Discharged at close of war. Age & poverty. Paid $60 1902-1905. Dead.
Deviso, Elizabeth	J. M. Deviso	L	Cobb's Legion	1862	John M. Kennedy	Surrendered Greensboro, North Carolina. Infirmity & poverty. Paid $60 1908-1910. Died 14 Jan 1910.
Fleming, Martha	W. W. Fleming	L	Cobb's Legion	Nov 1862	J. A. Fleming	Discharged Apr 1865. Infirmity & poverty. Paid $60 1907-1914.
Grizzard, Tabitha	Andrew Grizzard	A	48 Ga	1862	W. T. Roney, MD, J. C. Roley, S. R. Rayburn	Served until close of war. Infirmity & poverty. Paid $60 1902-1914. Married 1861.
Godowns, Elizabeth	Jno. M. Godowns	G	2 Ga	1864	W. W. Terrell, MD, W. T. Roney, W. R. Thompson	Home on furlough at end of war. Age & poverty. Paid $60 1902-1914. Married 1855.
Gordon, Mary	James Gordon	F	Cobb's		J. D. Wright, MD, L. C.	Indigent pensioner.

Widow	Husband	Co.	Regiment	Enl.	Witnesses	Notes
J.			Legion		Warren, S. J. Gordon	Paid $60 1903-1912. Died Feb 1912. Married 1856.
Grubbs, Rosa E.	B. A. Grubbs	C	1 Ga	1862		In hospital sick 1865. Died of rheumatism 1899. Paid $60 1903-1914. Married 1859.
Jordan, Nancy	James Jordan	F	8 Ga		J. W. Pilcher, MD, W. J. Rhodes, MD, J. C. Little	Served 2 years, 9 months. Age & poverty. Paid $60 1902-1907. Married 1854.
Jordan, Mattie E.	Captain J. P. Jordan	G	57 Ga		D. Harmon, W. M. English	Discharged Apr 1865. Infirmity & poverty. Paid $60 1907-1914. Married 1854.
McDonough, Hannah	Roger McDonough		Abel's Fla	1861	G. T. Brown, MD, C. W. Salter, A. J. Murat	Served until the close of war. Age & poverty. Paid $60 1903-1907. Married 1840.
McGahee, Frances A.	John M. McGahee	F	8 Ga Cav		Joel Guy, Thos. Peebles, S. F. Beasley	Infirmity & poverty. Paid $60 1908-1914.
Phillips, Mary V.	W. H. Phillips	A	48 Ga		L. O. Rohms, S. A. H. Thompson, Thos. Peebles	Infirmity & poverty. Paid $60 1905-1914.

Widow	Husband	Co.	Regiment	Enl.	Witnesses	Notes
Philips, Kiziah	Wm Philips	A	48 Ga		J. W. Pilcher, MD, W. H. Phelps, C. W. Salter, MD	Invalid pensioner. Infirmity & poverty. Paid $60 1905-1910. Died 10 Nov 1910. Married 1860.
Paradise, E. D.	W. D. Paradise				S. B. Tarver, W. P. Smith, P. Hubert, MD	Was indigent pensioner. Infirmity & poverty. Paid $60 1902-1910. Died 15 Dec 1910. Paid funeral $39.50. Married 1861.
Prescott, Oma	James Prescott	G	2 Ga		W. J. Rhodes, MD, J. J. Phillips, J. W. Pilcher, MD	Served 10 months. Discharged disability. Age & poverty. Paid $60 1902-1907. Married 1847.
Perdue, Margaret	Jackson Perdue	A 28	1864		C. H. Raley, MD, A. J. Williams	Home on sick furlough at close of war. Age & poverty. Paid $60 1907-1914. Married 1850.
Ponder, Elizabeth	J. G. Ponder					

Index

Oliver, 19
Olmstead, 19, 39
Oury, 45
Outten, 8, 153
Owen, 151
Owens, 134, 135
Oxford, 85, 89, 107, 110, 134, 135
Padgett, 29, 118
Page, 8, 40, 68, 80, 136, 137
Palmer, 42, 62, 72, 124
Pannell, 12, 19
Paradise, 46, 80, 137, 153, 158
Parish, 136
Parker, 9, 19, 83
Parkes, 8
Parsons, 9
Pate, 93
Patterson, 39
Peebles, 28, 37, 57, 58, 70, 136, 137, 157
Peel, 47, 145
Peeler, 28, 58
Peell, 4
Pendy, 44
Pennington, 94
Penrow, 39
Perdue, 9, 28, 34, 35, 57, 59, 83, 85, 93,
    134, 144, 152, 158
Perkins, 9, 28, 35, 50, 60, 153, 155
Perry, 19, 47
Pervis, 28, 35, 59
Phelps, 158
Philip, 83
Philips, 158
Phillips, 54, 72, 119, 124, 136, 143, 145,
    157, 158
Phillips, W. H., 124
Pickles, 130
Pilcher, 9, 128, 129, 133, 135, 136, 137,
    138, 139, 140, 141, 142, 157, 158
Poland, 4, 122, 125
Polhill, 4, 12, 44, 92, 94, 125, 145
Ponder, 49, 145, 158
Pool, 107, 124, 153
Pope, 19, 28, 44, 54, 67, 68, 83, 124, 136,
    141
Pophand, 28

Postin, 45
Potter, 151, 153
Pound, 94
Powell, 40, 42, 51, 90, 92, 94, 122, 127, 139
Prescott, 136, 158
Pugesley, 23, 28, 59
Pugesly, 33, 55
Pughesly, 48
Puler, 37
Purvis, 49, 51
Quincy, 42, 124, 138
Quinney, 50, 145, 146
Quinsey, 46
Rabun, 94
Raburn, 39, 62
Ragsdale, 28
Raiford, 41
Railey, 93
Raines, 9, 93
Rains, 48, 52, 145
Raley, 127, 128, 129, 130, 131, 132, 133,
    134, 136, 137, 139, 140, 141, 142, 153,
    158
Rayburn, 72, 123, 124, 130, 156
Rea, 135
Reagin, 131
Reese, 49, 52, 68, 98, 105, 137
Reeve, 106
Reeves, 98, 107, 108
Register, 20
Reid, 49, 153
Rereirister, 52
Reynolds, 44, 45, 138
Rhoder, 141
Rhodes, 46, 94, 122, 124, 128, 129, 130,
    131, 134, 137, 138, 139, 152, 153, 155,
    157, 158
Rickeson, 20
Ricks, 20
Rivers, 136, 143
Robbins, 48
Roberson, 9, 28, 37, 68, 137
Roberts, 9, 50, 79, 138, 145
Robinson, 28, 35, 59, 60, 153
Rodes, 135
Rogers, 9, 42, 43, 138

165

www.ingramcontent.com/pod-product-compliance
Lightning Source LLC
Chambersburg PA
CBHW061742270326
41928CB00011B/2340